The ART Is the CLOTH

The ART Is the CLOTH

HOW TO LOOK AT AND UNDERSTAND TAPESTRIES

MICALA SIDORE

FOREWORD BY CHARISSA BREMER-DAVID

4880 Lower Valley Road • Atglen, PA 19310

Other Schiffer Books on Related Subjects:

Anatomy of a Tapestry: Techniques, Materials, Care, Jean Pierre Larochette & Yadin Larochette, ISBN 978-0-7643-5933-0

Contemporary International Tapestry, Carol K. Russell, ISBN 978-0-7643-4869-3

Artistry in Fiber, Vol. 1: Wall Art, Anne Lee & E. Ashley Rooney, ISBN 978-0-7643-5304-8

Copyright © 2020 by Micala Sidore
Library of Congress Control Number: 2020930560

All rights reserved. No part of this work may be reproduced or used in any form or by any means—graphic, electronic, or mechanical, including photocopying or information storage and retrieval systems—without written permission from the publisher.

The scanning, uploading, and distribution of this book or any part thereof via the Internet or any other means without the permission of the publisher is illegal and punishable by law. Please purchase only authorized editions and do not participate in or encourage the electronic piracy of copyrighted materials.

"Schiffer," "Schiffer Publishing, Ltd.," and the pen and inkwell logo are registered trademarks of Schiffer Publishing, Ltd.

Designed by Ashley Millhouse
Cover design by Molly Shields
Front cover image: Cecilia Blomberg, *Hand to Hand*
Back cover images: Top row, l to r: Connie Lippert, *Wakulla* (detail), Photo: Chris Bartol. Peter Horn, *Von Wem ist denn das?* / *Who Did This?* (detail). Porfirio Gutierrez, *Celestial Space* (detail). Bottom row, l to r: Otavalo tapestry detail, 1970s. Alex Friedman, *Here Today* (detail). Elizabeth Radcliffe, *Marc Camille Chaimowicz* (detail).
Type set in Brandon Grotesque/GeoSlab703

ISBN: 978-0-7643-5992-7
Printed in China

Published by Schiffer Publishing, Ltd.
4880 Lower Valley Road
Atglen, PA 19310
Phone: (610) 593-1777; Fax: (610) 593-2002
E-mail: Info@schifferbooks.com
Web: www.schifferbooks.com

For our complete selection of fine books on this and related subjects, please visit our website at www.schifferbooks.com. You may also write for a free catalog.

Schiffer Publishing's titles are available at special discounts for bulk purchases for sales promotions or premiums. Special editions, including personalized covers, corporate imprints, and excerpts, can be created in large quantities for special needs. For more information, contact the publisher.

We are always looking for people to write books on new and related subjects. If you have an idea for a book, please contact us at proposals@schifferbooks.com.

To the community of tapestry weavers who
create such remarkable work and who have
shown me such generosity,

and to my lovely Bill Oram,
all day, every day.

On my loom there is a tapestry,
and in that tapestry there is my life.
In my life there are people
and memories and designs and colours and history.
And at the center of those things there are threads.
And in those threads there is a story.
And if you will listen I will tell you,
and then you will know.

—*Artist statement by Lorna Ramslochansingh*

CONTENTS

Foreword: Visual Poetry 9

Acknowledgments 10

Introduction 12

1. The Elements of Weaving 14

2. Special Materials 48

3. Visual Themes, Adapting the Past to the Present 64

4. Trompe l'oeil 92

5. Directionality 107

6. Textiles and Identities, When Textiles Define a Particular Group 134

7. Self-Reference 175

8. Historical Self-Reference 190

9. The Art in the Cloth 222

Amnézia/Amnesia
Zsu Zsa Péreli, 1980 | 60" × 40" | Wool, silk, gold thread
Szombatheley Gallery of Art, Hungary

Huipil de las Ideas
Luis Lazo, 2013 | 17.25" × 13" | Wool, silk; cotton warp

FOREWORD
Visual Poetry

In our three-dimensional world, tapestry can be optically perceived—and just as often dismissed—as flat and two-dimensional.

Tapestry is not flat. It is not two-dimensional, literally or metaphorically.

On the contrary, tapestry is rich and textured, tactile and visual.

It is woven of fiber, interlaced strand by strand, over and under, in a time-consuming process that simultaneously constructs both the physical cloth itself and the pattern. Though traditional tapestry weave is an ancient technique, it remains ever vibrant. Its possibilities are as boundless as human creativity.

Micala Sidore makes us stop in our tracks, in order to look and to see the visual poetry of the weavers' art. She takes us beyond the cursory glance, to mindful looking, to contemplation, to appreciation, to an understanding of the cloth.

She introduces us to a breadth of artists from around the globe, from the past to the here and now. She makes tapestry relevant. We reflect upon the perfect and imperfect work of the hand, the mind, and the heart.

Charissa Bremer-David
Los Angeles, California

ACKNOWLEDGMENTS

I thank the following:

Stan Sherer, photographer extraordinaire, who corrected my photographic mistakes and did all he could to ensure good-quality images;

Brigitte Hogan, who learned where I needed to send my inquiries in France—and corrected my French;

Andrea Hairston, who gave me a room in the theater building at Smith College, so I could give presentations of some chapters;

Anna Slezak, my friend and helper who, whether local or living 500 miles away, discussed many things with me and sent out permission forms to folks near and far;

James Emery and Mary Teichman, who helped me organize—and proofread;

My personal angels—Beth and Larry Beede, Julia Demmin, Steve Foster, Karen Jackson, Margaret and Larry Kornfeld, Pam Pier, Franz Riedel, Joe Wilhelm;

Joan Baxter, who introduced me to her group of Scottish tapestry weavers;

Cresside Collette, who threw a luncheon party at her home near Melbourne, Australia, so that I could meet some of the Oz tapestry community;

Lynne Curran, who had so many good ideas and suggestions;

Irina Dyatlovskaya, whose essay on Buryat horsehair tapestry weavers provided me invaluable insights, and who helped me remember the name of the Buryat weaver I had met, Bayarma Dambieva, so that I could meet her again; the travel agency MIR, especially Olga Hayes (in the US) and Natasha Suzdalnitskaya (in Ulan Ude, Siberia), who found several more horsehair tapestry weavers for me to meet and talk with, and then later tracked them down to gather more information that I needed about their work; and Martha Borawski, travel agent, who helped me organize my trips;

Annika Ekdahl, who suggested possible contributors;

Ibolya Hegyi (now deceased and much missed) and her husband, Laçi Valy, who discussed my ideas and connected me with the right Hungarian institutions and their tapestry holdings;

Masako Ishidate, from Kobe, Japan, who traveled with me in search of tapestry weavers and fiber artists around Kobe, Kyoto, and Sapporo;

Elzbièta Kędzia, who introduced me to many Polish fiber artists and has always supported me and my tapestry work;

Jean Pierre Larochette, who introduced me to Zapotec weavers;

Maximo Laura, who introduced me to tapestry weavers in the Wari tradition in the city of Ayacucho, Peru;

Dana Leibsohn, who always knows lots—and shares it with such grace;

Ulrikka Mokdad, who helped me research some of the historical images and suggested other Danish tapestry weavers;

Jacques Postel (now deceased and much missed) and Jean Claude Lagrange, who taught me so much about all aspects of tapestry at la Manufacture Nationale des Gobelins;

Joanne Soroka, who made suggestions and, when I visited Edinburgh, gave a dinner party to which she invited several members of the local tapestry community.

In addition, I thank the following administrators and gallery directors, who provided venues for the original exhibition of *The Art Is the Cloth*:

New Hampshire Institute of Art, Manchester, New Hampshire / Patrick McCay (the original supporter of my idea); George School, Newtown, Pennsylvania / Amedeo Salamoni; and Deerfield Academy, Deerfield, Massachusetts / Lydia Hemphill.

I thank also my parents, who always insisted I could and would find my niche.

Finally, I thank my friends and family in my version of crowd sourcing, each of whom contributed $20 apiece—and sometimes more (!)—toward the expense of acquiring images from museums and other institutions.

INTRODUCTION

This book does not present a definitive account of tapestry. Rather, it attempts to show how certain tapestries reflect back on what they are: pieces of cloth. For many years I have been thinking about the ways that they do this, and searching for examples. My choices have a certain amount of happenstance about them. Much of what I have been able to include came about because of my travels. In the fall of 2015, for instance, I arranged to visit with Buryats in Siberia, so that I could see their horsehair tapestries.

My travels have provided me with both blessings and limitations. At times I include brilliant work that comes from traditions outside my own expertise. And then there are the frustrations of space. There are many terrific tapestries for which there was no room here, including other pieces made by artists whom I do include. There are also many tapestries, just as successful, that fall outside the scope of this project.

Above all, in this book, I wish to provide strategies for looking. People are sometimes overwhelmed by the size of historical tapestry, or by its odd imagery, or by its faded colors, or perhaps simply by the realization that such objects are handwoven. They can miss the opportunity to see fully, and so to appreciate, what these works of art have to offer. Here I present a variety of suggestions to help people see—and I also introduce readers to some of the truly spectacular makers out there.

After a brief discussion of technical matters (chapter 1), the following chapters suggest ways in which tapestries speak to the art of cloth-making. The seven ways are not mutually exclusive, and many of the tapestries might just as validly have appeared in two or even three different chapters. I've tried throughout to include many variations within these categories.

The idea for this book may have begun when Helena Hernmarck sent me a fax that read "The art is the cloth," or when Archie Brennan reminded his students repeatedly that tapestry *is* a piece of cloth, or when Silvia Heyden talked with me about her *loomish* eyes. She saw the world around her as an endless resource that she would weave into tapestries. She kept discovering more rhythms, more ways to make the warp and weft work with each other. These three master weavers have opened up spaces for me to think about what I am doing, both as a weaver and as a writer who hopes to help others see.

Micala Sidore
Northampton, Massachusetts

One
THE ELEMENTS OF WEAVING

Not Wet Either
Linda Hutchins, 1995 | 3" × 18.25" | Cotton seine twine, map pins

Weaving a tapestry involves multiple decisions.

The design is not a matter independent of the weaving, but deeply integrated into the process of making. What weight warp? What weight weft? Will the weaving be weft-faced, or will both warp and weft show?

Will the warp be visible at the ends, be tucked up into the hem, or will it appear in the body of the tapestry? Will the weaving be *plain weave*, as in the sample here, or more complex—a twill, a rose path, a brocade—or something else? Will the surface be flat, textured, or dimensional? Will the completed piece be rectangular, square, or something else entirely?

Will the thread be solid colors or a mixture? Will the mixing of yarns, sizes and colors, be random or calculated? For some makers, the dye stuff matters enormously. Will they use organic materials or chemicals?

Will they employ a dyeing system like ikat? Will they lay paint on the threads?

The pieces in this section of the book dramatize those decisions, and more. Always, what the weaver makes is a piece of cloth.

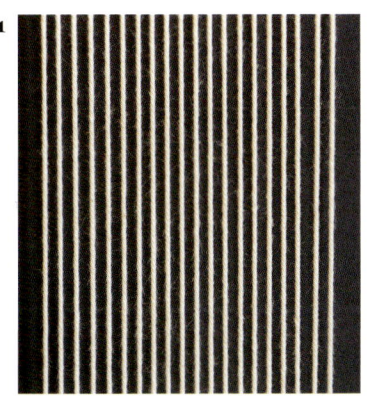

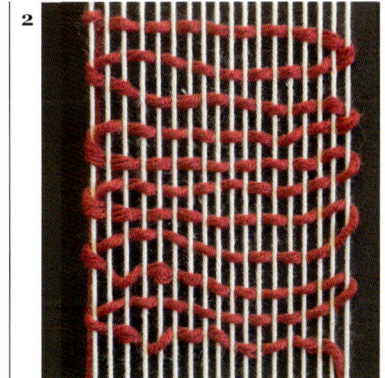

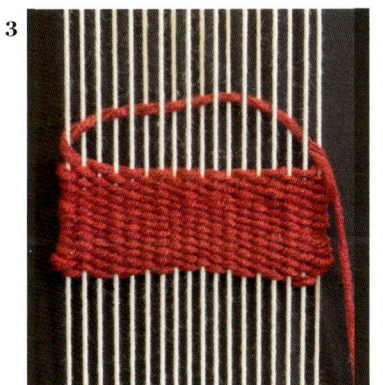

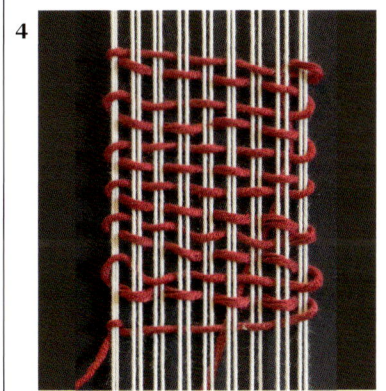

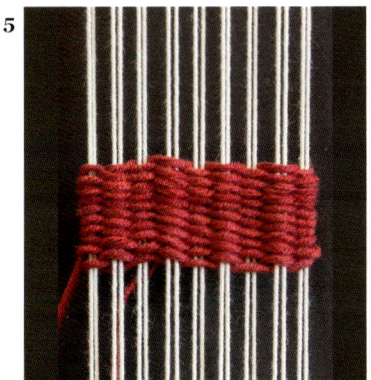

Warp and weft: weaving basics

1. The vertical warp

2. The warp interlaced by weft, one thread at a time

3. The weft tamped down over warp, producing a textile called weft faced (single seed)

4. The warp interlaced by weft, two threads at a time

5. The weft tamped down over warp, producing a weft-faced textile (double seed)

LINE

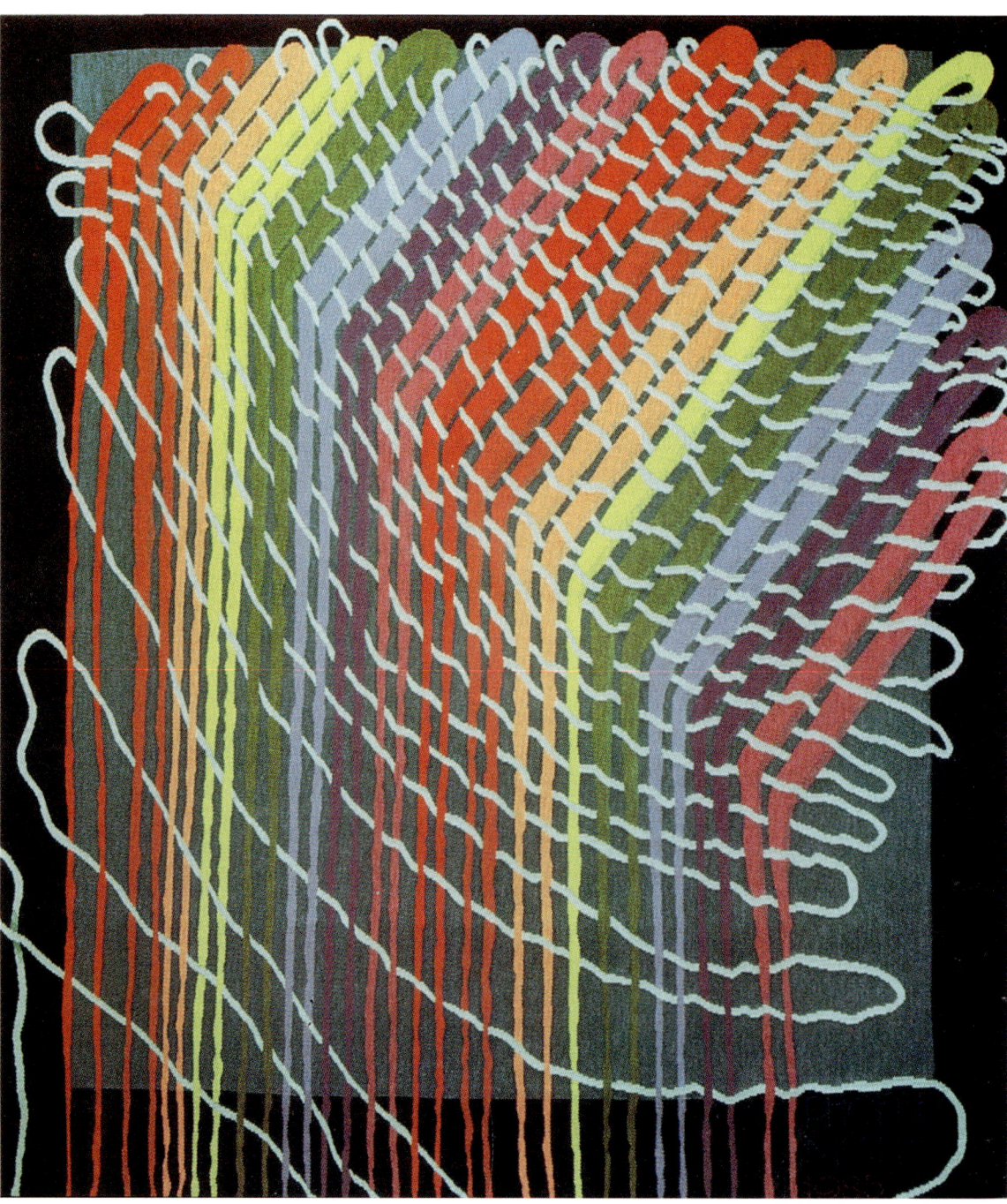

Fibril
Phoebe McAfee, 1985 | 6'4" × 5'5" | Wool; cotton seine twine warp

McAfee is making her piece with a subtext: what she weaves exemplifies what she is doing, a tapestry showing threads interlacing other threads.

Stoff meines (deutschen) Lebens / The Fabric of My (German) Life
Thomas Cronenberg, 2000 | 4' × 5'10" | Cotton, mercerized cotton, linen (various), viscose, silk; cotton warp

Weaving a line can be a simple thing—weft back and forth, over and under from left to right, followed by under and over from right to left.

Cronenberg produces innumerable variations amid a seemingly simple design—thicks and thins, x's of all sorts.

Number One
Margaret Jones, 2013 | 36.6" × 47.25" | Wool, rayon, silk; cotton warp

Weaving a short black line into a field of white is straightforward and simple. But the result opens up speculations about what one sees: the areas of white and black are pure, but then, toward the middle, a short black bit, which seems to bleed into the white.

In Rhythm with the Moon and Tides
Leila Thomson, 2017 | 20" × 14" | Linen, cotton, rayon

Every time the weft crosses in front of the warp, it produces a *seed* of color. The seed is comparable to a pixel on a computer screen. When the weaver, as Thomson does here, varies what she interlaces—either single warps or double warps—seeds change size. This is visible, for instance, in the shoreline, where larger seeds grow smaller to the right. The single seed area produces a finer surface.

SLITS

Warp threads run in parallel lines.

For instance, if one weaves warps 1–5 together, and then, with a separate thread, warps 6–10, then that creates a gap between warps 5 and 6. This gap is known technically as a slit.

Where Two Tides Meet
Fiona Hutchison, 2006 | 47.2" × 44.5" | Linen, cotton, paper, monofilament yarn; cotton warp
Photo: Michael Wolchover

Hutchison takes advantage of the slits between warp threads as she weaves bands. The eye can see the slit as a fine line. These narrow bands will move slightly when the work is hung. At the bottom, Hutchison lays in random threads.

It looks like foam. The waters are troubled.

Ambiguous Deliberations
Line DuFour, 1989 | 8' × 20' | Wool, silk, miscellaneous fibers

DuFour's bands pull away from each other when she hangs the tapestry. She has woven across the entire width at the top and bottom, so the whole remains one piece of cloth with immensely long slits.

WARP

The most common tapestry is weft faced, with the warp unseen except perhaps as ribs along the surface of the cloth. But not always. The warp may appear as fringe. And in constructing a piece of cloth, the maker may leave the warp visible as a design element within the whole.

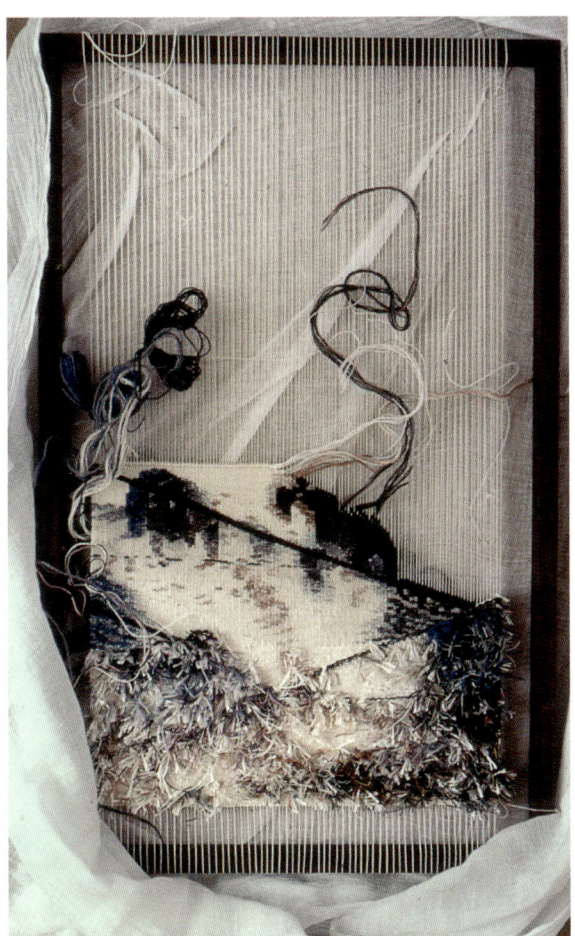

The Petworth Maid
Pat Taylor, 1996 | 11.8" × 6.3" | Silk, wool | Photo: Pat Taylor

Commissioned to make a tapestry for a country manor in England, Taylor created this *maid* in a state meant to look unfinished. With trailing threads and curly hair, restrained within the frame, she lies in a drawer (lined with a sheet) in the kitchen.

Indigo Bath
Sarah Swett, 2003 | 48" × 28" | Wool

A mass of warp threads line up across the width of the tapestry, almost like rain, as the figure rinses herself.

Blood Cannot Be Washed Out with Blood
Unn Sonju, 2010 | 9'2" × 8'2" | Wool

Wefts like blood pool amid warps.

It's all red.

Life Interrupted
Inge Norgaard, 2001 | 14" × 18" | Wool, plastic from water bottles, plastic sewing thread; cotton seine twine warp

Norgaard decided that the warp would show, and the bottom would be ragged, left incomplete. Three of her friends had come down with breast cancer during one spring. She saw how surreptitious cancer can be, resembling cloth moths (in plastic), eating away at the weft.

System IV
Cos Ahmet, 2016 | 8.3" × 11.4" | Linen, mercerized cotton, nylon filament; linen and cotton warp

Ahmet has created a kind of netting, weaving and not weaving in the construction of this piece. A hint of spiderwebs.

Photo Revelation
Elke Hülse, 2015 | 42.5" × 35.8" | Photo paper, fabric strips, cotton

Some of the photographic sections of Hülse's piece are actual photographs, inserted between warps, drawing attention to the difference between what is woven and what is shot by a camera.

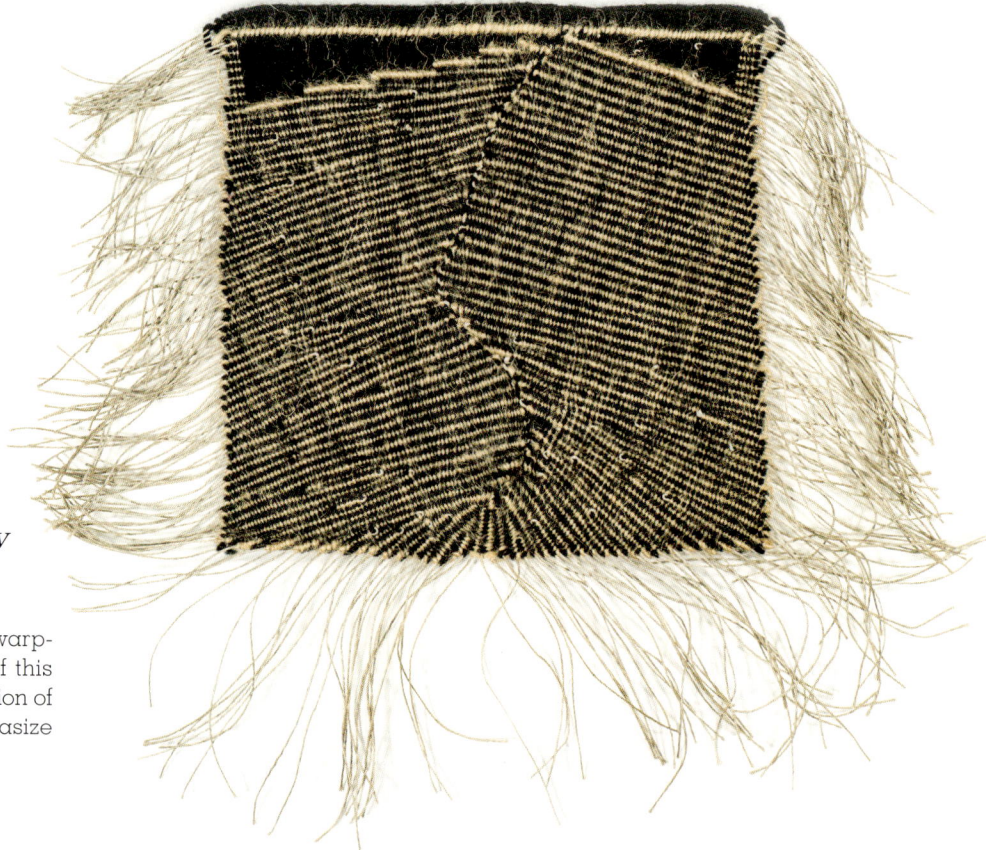

The Sketch for Proverbs IV
Włodzimierz Cygan, 2004 | 8" × 8" (woven part) | Wool, sisal

Cygan has long played with warp-based designs. Every part of this image comes from the direction of the warp, splayed out to emphasize the process of weaving.

Grampians Snapshot
Cathy Hoffman, late 1980s | approx. 28" × 28" | Wool; cotton warp

The mountains near Hoffman's home in Australia. She attached miniatures to the surface, like snapshots in a scrapbook.

SHAPE

A minimum of two warp threads, one odd and one even, can produce something substantial, something real, cloth as narrow as a band—or (with more warps) as wide as the widest loom. Some of the following makers have taken full advantage of that.

An irregular uneven edge is also possible.

The Tapestry Machine
Christine Sawyer, 2013 | 11" × 6" | Cotton, metal | (metal structure fabricated by David Sawyer)

Sometimes, the process of making can feel like a sausage machine—everything goes in and something emerges.

Folded Loss I
Jacy Wall, 2013, remade in 2016 | 47.25" × 19.7" | Stitch wool; cotton warp

Exploiting the physical nature of tapestry—folding, shaping, cutting, sewing together. Is the whole a figure? Single eye, open mouth? Is that diagonal line a scar?

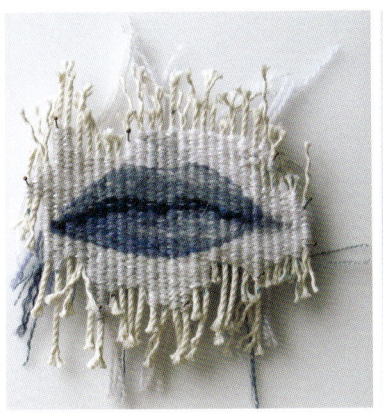 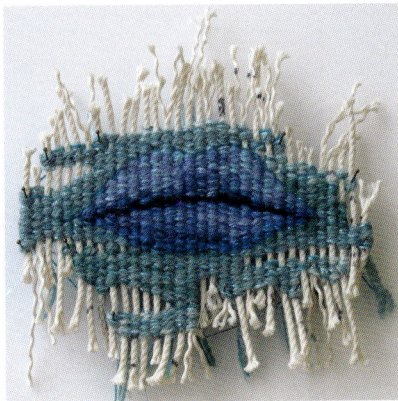 

Mots Glacés, Mots Noyés, Mots Voilés / Frozen Words, Drowned Words, Veiled Words
Suzanne Paquette, 2009 | 7.9" × 7.9" (each) | Wool, cotton, synthetic

A visual metaphor. Also—warp fringe as a border.

Exploding Mummy Bundle
Marge Puryear, 1985–86 | 15" × 15" | Handspun and dyed linen, handspun Jacob's sheep wool, mounted on linen with silk stitching

This is woven to show both warp and weft, and Puryear celebrates the material and the wild results. One might note how she deals with the hair.

The Chorus
Liv Pedersen, 2016 | 27.5" × 42.5" | Wool, synthetics; cotton warp

Pedersen uses rya technique, best known for rugs, to make her large population of individuals.

Huff 'n Puff and Shake 'n Quake
Becky Stevens, 2014 | 10.25" × 9" | Wool; cotton and wire warp | and 10.75" × 9.75" | Wool; cotton warp

Shaped pieces lean and overbalance, evoking atmospheric and geologic instability.

Morbihan Menhir
Mary Kester, 2016 | 58" × 32" × 3" | Wool, cotton

Kester makes several layers of cloth all from the same warp. She uses the various parts, as well as shading and color, to construct pieces that are shaped and highly three-dimensional.

Butterflies
Yasuko Fujino, 2007 | 4.3" × 3.5" × 1.1" each (5 of 100) | Silk, metal thread, mohair | Photo: Makato Yano

Fujino exhibits these pieces individually in wooden frames, covered by glass. They look like specimens in a natural history museum.

Horizon, Atlantic
Susan Iverson, 1997 | 1'8.5" × 5'2" × 5" | Linen, silk; linen warp | Avenir Museum, Colorado State University

Iverson adds extra length to certain warp threads in order to create the white shapes. The final result looks like a curtain rising in a theater.

La Doña
Christine Laffer, 2014 | 30" × 24" × 5" | Wool, alpaca, silk, linen

Laffer has long been intrigued by the visual effects of weaving with a weft that pulls the warp out of plumb—which occurs when the weft is not woven at a 90-degree angle to the warp. At les Gobelins in Paris, this is called *eccentric weft*; in the US, the technique is called *pulled warp* or *wedge weave*. Laffer has taken full advantage of all that warp.

Inspiration
Monique Chmielewska Lehman, 2016 | 8'4" × 3'4" × 4'4" | Silk, rayon, wool; cotton warp, synthetic net

Lehman changed the warp direction daily.

From Above
Silvia Heyden, 2014 | 40" × 42" | Linen, silk, wool

Silvia Heyden described herself as a *naughty weaver*, in that her style of weaving was untraditional. Her completed pieces have irregular surfaces and edges. She referred to her own body, since, for years, the spread of her arms defined the width of her tapestries; the distance between the base of her palm and the top of her middle finger defined smaller elements within the whole.

A Weaverly Path (last, uncompleted tapestry)
Silvia Heyden, 2014 | 35" × 39.5" | Linen, silk, wool

No one can know where the threads would have taken Heyden with this final unfinished piece. The hand is always visible in what she wove.

Her book, *The Making of Modern Tapestry*, has become a classic.

WEAVING TECHNIQUES

The best-known tapestry weave is a plain weave: over and under, one thread at a time. But this is not the only way to weave a tapestry. Complex weaves offer other possibilities, other surfaces.

Shawl, India, Kashmir, late 18th–early 19th century
40.5" × 45.25" | Wool twill tapestry | Boston Museum of Fine Arts

Shawl weavers in Kashmir continue to make these. The twill weave produces a diagonal line, visible when the surface is closely examined.

Aurora at Sea
Pam Patrie, 2009 | 8.5" × 8.5" |
Silk, antique gold thread

Patrie emphasizes the vertical warps in the center, and the diagonals of twill in the border/frame.

Monochrome Texture: Rouen Facade
Alta Turner, 2013 | 11" × 7" × 0.5" | Cotton, metallics; cotton seine twine warp | Photo: Nancy Dosko

Turner takes Monet's subject—a cathedral door—and suggests light and texture by differing materials and techniques.

Rebecca 2
Judy Schuster, 1985 | 18" × 28" | Hand-dyed wool; linen warp | Featured in AFI Video *Weaver's Cloth*

Schuster takes advantage of the odd-and-even structure of plain weave to create two faces, one whiter, in the middle, each embedded in the other.

Ikon
Geary Jones, 2004–2005 | 16" × 22" (without frame) | Cotton tatting yarn | Frame, 2009 | Acrylic, gloss gel medium

Jones's use of the technique *soumak* produces a slightly knobbly surface. All those faces.

The technique: A weft thread circles each warp thread before moving on to the next. Then, to give greater stability, the weaver inserts two lines of plain weave before the next row of *soumak*.

Including and painting the frame he wove on is simply fun, continuing the discussion of the content between two media.

(The gray is the wall behind the tapestry.)

Impression. Night-Day
Feliksas Jakubauskas, 2009 | 4' 3" × 5'11" (× 2) | Wool, viscose, silk | Mixed Gobelins technique with streak weaving

Streak weaving, for Jakubauskas, consists of those parts of a tapestry where he links various seeds at angles and thus extends lines of a single color. He has created a sense of both surface and depth.

EMBROIDERY

A way to embellish a surface.

Unhinged 2
Sarah Haskell, 2015 | 40" × 48" | Hand-dyed brocade woven linen; rayon, woven paper, buttons

The brocade weave that Haskell creates with linen produces a surface irregular to the touch. The figure is embroidered.

Circle of Leaves
Barbara Eckhardt, 1995 | 38" × 45" | Cotton, linen, ramie; interlocking supplementary warps, weft inlay, embroidery

Eckhardt wove at a loom where she could produce as many as six layers at the same time (she chose to work with only three layers): a complex single piece of fabric emerged. Then she added embroidery (the birds, for sure).

COLOR

One can work with individual colors, or combine colors, or play with the organization of the threads. Some colors are more unstable than others. Purple, for instance, fades and shifts quickly.

Black on Black
Marilyn Rea-Menzies, 2004 | 5.9" × 5.9" (× 12) | Cotton, wool, chenille, linen, plastic, metallic

Each section provides another variation of contrast, texture, techniques—and legibility.

White on White
Moik Schiele, 1974 | 15.4" × 7.3" | Wool, linen, silk, mercerized cotton, synthetic and silver thread | Gift of Mildred Constantine | Cleveland Art Museum

White is an unreliable color. The fiber matters. White cotton, for instance, is much whiter than white wool, which, if bleached white, would disintegrate. Over time, as well, all whites yellow. Variations of white and off-white fill the weaving—and will probably continue to shift in tone over time.

SUBTLETY AND PRECISION

Below: ***Leurs Esprits s'enfonçaient désordonnés / Their Spirits Sank into Disarray***

Left: Detail.

Marcel Marois, 1988–89 | 5'6" × 10'3" | Wool; cotton warp | Collection: Lotto-Quebec Montreal

Marois works with bundles of weft, which he places with great exactness in order to emphasize one thread or another.

Black Verticals with Linen Field
Sara Brennan, 2001 | 22" × 19" | Linen, cotton, sewing thread

The linen and cotton will reflect light differently.

Galaxy II
Ibolya Hegyi, 1994 | 39.4" × 39.4" | Wool, metallic thread

Photographs of Hegyi's work fail to show the rich specific detail she lavished on each. In this rendering of the galaxy, she treated her subject with precision.

IKAT AND PAINT

Ikat is a technique (originating in Indonesia) in which warp or weft threads, or both, are dyed before weaving. It is akin to tie-dye.

Dwelling
Mary Kirchner, 2014 | 25" × 21" | Cotton; weft ikat

Because Kirchner has used ikat to dye the weft, many edges have shadows. Then she incorporates three clean verticals—the black upright and the left side of the gray-green shape.

Sun and Shield

Polly Barton | 31" × 32" | Handwoven silk; double (warp and weft) ikat, with additional painted pigment and soy milk on the warp

A very comprehensive way of using ikat.

Right: *P. Kasuri No. 207*
Jun Tomita, 2007 | 6'8" × 3'4.5" | Silk | Photo: Makoto Yano

Below: Detail.

Tomita has written a book about ikat and uses it regularly in his own work. The close-up shows the careful preparation and results.

Blueprint 7
Mary Zicafoose, 2009 | 7' × 7'2" | Resist-wrapped dyed woven wool; linen warp | Weft-faced ikat triptych | Photo: Kirby Zicafoose

Before she began, Zicafoose had to conceive of the whole of these fingerprints. The sections show even more about her skill at assembling one image from three parts.

Toward a Quiet Place
Betty Vera, 2007 | 14" × 16" | Cotton, painted warp | Photo: D. James Dee

Vera paints the warp before she mounts it on the loom, producing a random intersection of colors. Her surface also includes sporadic floating threads.

FINISHING AND DISINTEGRATING

Tapestries can last hundreds of years. Or maybe not. Here are two pieces making use of what is unfinished, and exploring the tapestry's resilience.

Amnézia/Amnesia
Zsu Zsa Péreli, 1980 | 60" × 40" | Wool, silk, gold thread
Szombatheley Gallery of Art, Hungary

In the process of weaving, as the weaver finishes with one color and begins with another, sometimes they will conceal the extraneous thread within the body of the work. Often, though, they leave threads trailing off the back.

Pérelli has it both ways; one sees two sides of a single tapestry with a provocative subtext.

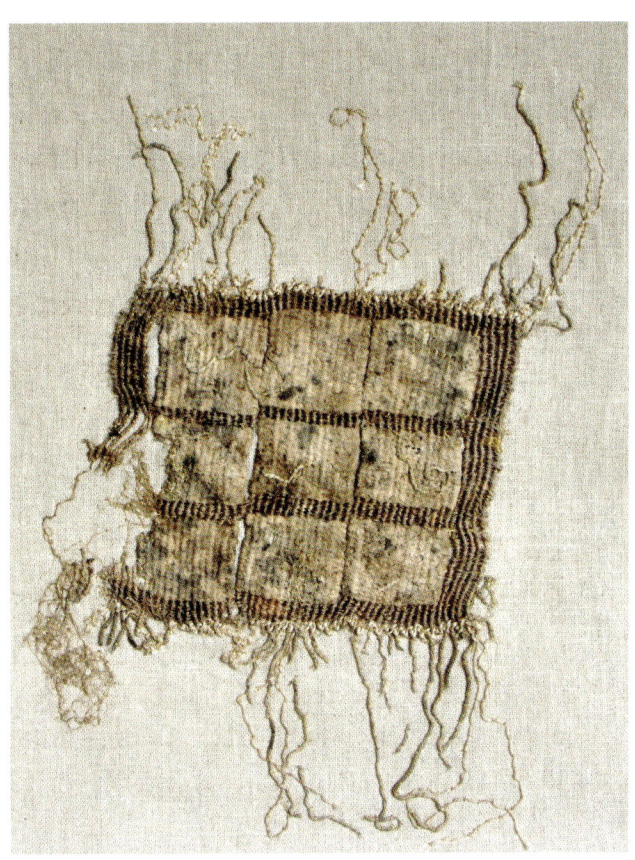

Unraveling the Constructed Boundaries
Dorothy Clews, 2014 | 18.1" × 10.2" | Linen, cotton, chenille, gold metallic thread, sewing thread; seine twine warp

Clews grew fascinated with the idea of how long tapestries survive. So, she began to bury her work in her garden, digging it up months later to see how it had seasoned.

Two
SPECIAL MATERIALS

What does it feel like?

Wool, cotton, linen, silk, rayon, polyester, bamboo, sisal, hemp, coconut, raffia, wool fleece, camelid fibers, goat's hair, horsehair, yak hair, dog hair, feathers, human hair, unspun animal hair, grasses, flowers, bark, leaves, beads, gold, silver, barbed wire, metal strips, buttons, shells, brooches, safety pins, photographic film, paper, pages from books, paper pulp, ribbon, gingham and other patterned cloth, in strips . . .

BURYATS

The Buryats of Siberia have long used horsehair in their nomadic life: for robes and harnesses, saddle girths, reins, fetters, and collars for horses and calves. The Buryats have also used it to weave mats, called taars, which have had many purposes both inside and outside the home.

The range of colors in horsehair is limited—black, grays, browns, and white, with white being the rarest. Horsehair can be dyed, but not easily, because the hair is both coarse and resistant to dyes. Buryat don't dye horsehair, and instead vary how they spin it and which part of the horse's hair they use.

The making of Buryat tapestry began in the 1970s in a revival of interest in folk culture, and took on greater energy in the 1980s. The work continues, though at a much reduced pace.

Creation
Alla Tsybiskova, designer, and Bayarma Dambieva, weaver, 1983 | 6'3" × 4'7" | Horsehair

SPECIAL MATERIALS

By the Old Tree
Bayarma Dambieva, 2011 | 33.8" × 25.2" | Horsehair

Dambieva considers this her finest work. It shows immense skill in the choices among subtly different tones.

Dangina
Bayarma Dambieva, 2014 | 19.7" × 11.8" | Horsehair, barrettes

Something of a visual pun—like a horse's mane or tail.

Toward the Wind
Tatyana Badueva, 2014 | 29.5" × 15.75" | Horsehair, yak hair

Compare with the above piece. Again, the woman's hair is like a horse's mane.

Generations
Tatyana Dashieva, 2012 | 51.2" × 23.6" | Horsehair

Close examination shows that while some of the faces are full on, the child's shows a profile too.

OTHER PIECES ROOTED IN GEOGRAPHY

Terra
Sue Lawty, 2005 | 2'3.5" × 6'6.5" | Hemp, linen, silk, wool

Lawty has described how her first visits to Australia, in the late 1980s, changed her approach to tapestry, introducing her to the earth pigment ocher and its range of colors for dyeing.

This piece has the look of pastures and worked agricultural land, such as one might see from an airplane. But Lawty is a rock person—she sees her tapestry as deeply geologic.

Roots Tapestry
Teresa-India Young, 1976 | 38.5" × 28.5" | Raffia | Courtesy of Jacqueline L. McRath | Photo: Amy Fink

Raffia originates in Africa. The surface here, covered with a kind of long fringe—part of the weft—gives the impression of dreadlocks.

Red I
Alastair Duncan, 1998 | 21.6" × 18.1" × 1.4" | Cotton, wool, barbed wire; cotton warp

During "the Troubles," Duncan studied at the University of Belfast, Northern Ireland. He saw barbed wire everywhere, and so it became a logical material, something sharp, for him to incorporate into his blood-red work.

Granite Lace
Margaret Sunday, 2007 | 24.5" × 12.5" | Cotton, linen, silk, synthetic threads, silk ribbons

Sunday celebrates textures in this tapestry, which for her recalls a place she has visited often from her home in Colorado.

AND ON TO OTHER STUFF:

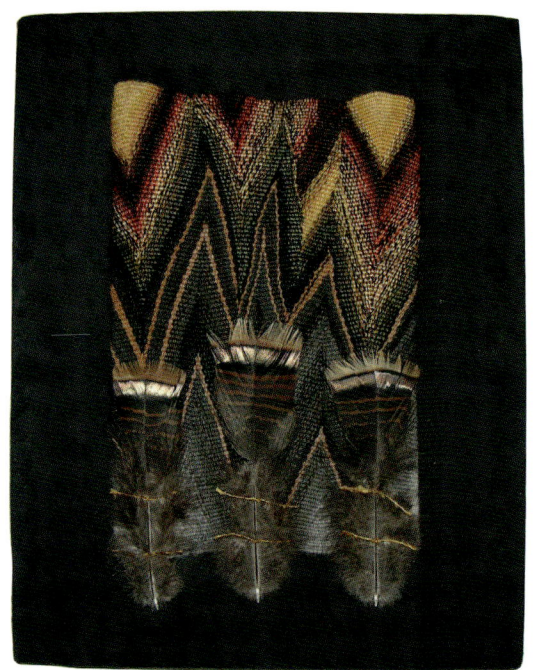

Wild Turkey
Sharon Crary, 2013 | 17.5" × 13.5" | Wool, cotton, turkey feathers

The feathers are delightfully extravagant.

Salas Federales / Covergence Diptych
Lilia Breyter, 2008 | 36.2" × 9" (× 2) | Copper thread, copper strips, fire oxidation

Copper dominates. The fire has made for variations in the color. It creates an energy like combustion. Layers of copper warp alternate with woven areas.

BCS News
Woiciech Jaskólka, 1996 | 14" × 12" | Cotton, wool, poliamid fiber, copper

Jaskólka has made many pieces with the word "news" in the title; some hint at the daily newspaper. The use of copper differs in its look from the previous tapestry.

Aurora
Rebecca Smith, 2014 | 11" × 15" × 3" | Mixed fibers, beads, wire; wire warp | Photo: Steve Rossman

The wire warp permits the shaping. Smith has made several pieces of this type, some of which look like bustiers.

Notes on a Black Book
Heidi Gassner, 1989 | 27.5" × 27.5" | Monofilament, strips of pages from old books

Gassner began with a grid of monofilament. She inserted the paper strips to make the writing and shapes. This work creates illusions: the viewer imagines a sheet of paper, with extravagant writing.

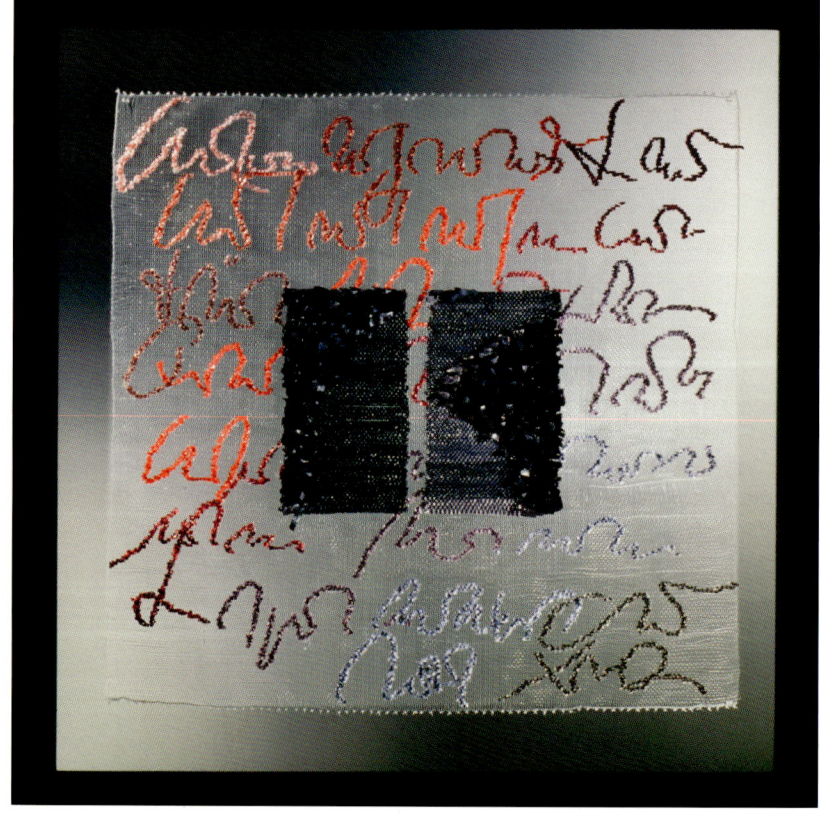

B + Y = Green
Maria Kovacs, 2012 | 19" × 13" × 1.25" | Recycled plastic bags; cotton warp

Kovacs devoted her work as an artist to ecological concerns.

This piece is stiff and has ridges because of the materials she used and the way she wove them.

Book of Golden Thoughts
Krystyna Sadej, 2016 | 6'11" × 5'7" × 7.9"–11.8" | Recycled plastic foil, garbage bags, synthetic/metallic yarns; video tape warp | Photo: Gregory Abnaszko

The piece holds its shape—and is extremely lightweight. It can be waved—sounding like autumn leaves being crushed.

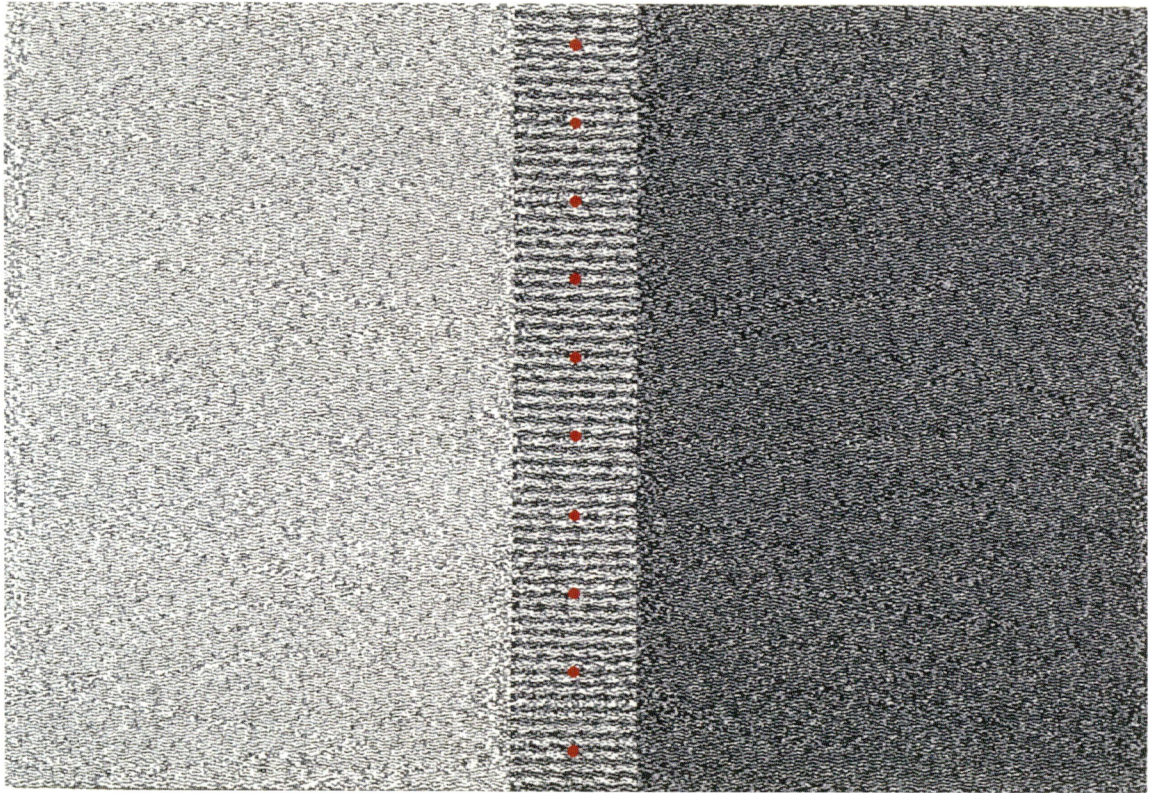

In-Between #2
Sara Lindsay, 1999 | 4' × 5'11" | Cotton | Collection: Ararat Regional Art Gallery, Australia | Photo: Simon Cuthbert

Lindsay has made a group of tapestries by using strips of gingham, a checked fabric, white with another color. Woven into a tapestry, gingham produces a surface with many variations.

Arid Landscape I
Ann Naustdal, 2009 | 53.1" × 57.1" | Linen, coco fiber, gold leaf | Photo: Kim Müller

The title directs the viewer to *arid*. The top section offers an image of a finely woven close-up—it might be cactus, the middle a desert landscape, and, at the bottom, coco fiber creates what could be underground, an area inhabited by worms.

for Irena Sendler
Joanne Soroka, 2015 | 4'–4'2" × 6'1" | Wool, linen, metallic thread, cotton, ash keys (seeds of the ash tree)

Soroka wanted to represent the life of Irena Sendler, who helped smuggle 2,500 children and infants out of the Warsaw Ghetto during World War II. Each ash key represents one life saved, painted gold because each life is valuable.

Tapestry Woman
Sandy Webster, 1994 | 13" × 6.5" | Raffia, tapa cloth, yarn, beads, willow

Webster is a relentless maker. She uses whatever is at hand to make what she can. This piece also recalls basket making.

Babes in Arms
Jon Eric Riis, 2001 | 5'7" × 2'4" × 1'6" (× 3) | Silk with leather and couched coral beads

Adult human size, the babes might look like paper dolls or punching bags with sand at the bottom. But they hold some disturbing accessories.

Gina

Joanne Sanburg, ca. 2000–2009 | 28" × 24"

One of a series of portraits that Sanburg wove, embellished with many materials: jewelry, curtain pulls, buttons, fake fur, shells, men's silk ties.

She further emphasized varieties of skin tones and layers of skin.

Boy Punk / Girl Punk

Candace Bahouth, 1980 | 25.6" × 31.9" × 3.9" (each) | Applied fabric, nylon bristles, pin badge, safety pins, metal chains, other mixed media and found objects; tapestry woven

Bahouth's vivid portraits, crammed with appropriate accessories. A pin on the girl reads GIRLS ARE POWERFUL. The artist first saw her subjects in a tea shop.

Three
VISUAL THEMES, ADAPTING THE PAST TO THE PRESENT

This chapter considers some of the ways that the artistic traditions of the past reappear in present-day tapestries.

Among the largest group, and, really, the most familiar group of tapestry-woven textiles, are area rugs, such as kilims and dhurries. Weavers see much in the basics of these pieces: a sequence of stripes or geometric shapes, particular techniques such as the Navajo wedge weave, the use of colors—hues and variations of hues.

Then, inspired, some weavers find a template for what they wish to create in their own work.

PLAYING WITH STRIPES AND ZIGZAGS

Navajo (Diné) / Shoulder Blanket with Plain-Stripe Design, 1860–90
5'10" × 4'1.5" | Wool; plain weave | twined warp ends and selvages; knotted corner tassels | Bequest of Alan R. Brodie | Chicago Art Institute

Stripes in brilliant colors alternate with wider passages, creating a rhythm.

Regular Horizontals I
Cornelia Theimer Gardella, 2011 | 18" × 27" | Hand-dyed wool; cotton warp | Private collection, Germany

One of Gardella's studies of stripes. The individual stripes are the same height and width, so color and sequence, from pale to rich, carry the story.

Quercus, or, A Carpet Bed
Stanley Bulbach, 2011 | 6' × 3' | Longwood Lincoln (sheep breed) wool, vegetal dyes

In this tapestry, the abstract patterning includes a representational element. *Quercus* is in the genus of the beech family, and Bulbach associates what he has woven with the woods—where snow falls gently onto oak leaves. The fringe has patterns too. The weaver takes great care in the sources of his wool, how he processes it, and how he dyes it.

Solar Flare
Robin Reider, 2010 | 55" × 40" | Hand-dyed wool (madder root, marigold, onion skins, cota, gumweed, chamisa, osage, peace leaves, chemical dyes)

Pairs of blue stripes in various tones alternating with shapes in a field of desert yellow. Reider acquires many of her dyestuffs locally, in New Mexico.

Neon Curves and Rectangles
Donna Loraine Contractor, 2015 | 5'8" × 3'4" | Wool

Contractor works in series, weaving several separate pieces across the width of her loom. Here her stripes go wonky, so that she can show something like a window frame, like a cityscape, like stained glass. (She has included several frames, which create the illusion of distance.)

Navajo Wedge Weave, 1885–90
5'11" × 4'7" | Wool | Fred Harvey Fine Arts Collection | Heard Museum, Phoenix, AZ | Photo: Craig Smith

Sometimes in a wedge weave—though it's not true of this piece—the weft pulling the warp out of plumb produces a scalloped edge and an irregular surface.

Wakulla
Connie Lippert, 2011 | 32" × 24" | Wool; linen warp, natural dyes | Photo: Chris Bartol

Lippert weaves wedge weave pieces exclusively. Both this and the next tapestry show dramatic scalloped edges. Lippert writes that she remembers visiting Wakulla County, Florida, as a child.

Fire Water
Deborah Corsini, 2016 | 46" × 34" | Wool, silk

Another landscape, more wedge weave. A major shift of color and style halfway down. One can see the progress of the weaver's work, a series of discoveries, a narrative.

Long Night over the Canyon
Sarah Warren, 2016 | 38" × 36" | Hand-dyed wool; cotton warp | Photo: Michael Walsh

Wedge weave with a dramatic change of color: a landscape of land and sky.

Journey II
Priscilla Alden, 2014 | 35" × 24" | Wool, hand-dyed

Each separate colored section works like a sawtooth, back and forth, proceeding up the height of the piece. The technique is akin to *lazy lines*.

Alden's blues in her lightning bolt add dramatically to her overall narrative.

VISUAL THEMES IN HISTORICAL TAPESTRIES

Some weavers highlight the visual conventions found in historical tapestries: greenery (*verdure, mille fleurs*) and the use of borders. In both, the look and size depend on where and when the tapestry was woven.

VERDURES, MILLE FLEURS, GREENERY

***Mille fleurs*, 1530–45**
Belgium | 11'6" × 13'1" | Wool, silk | Gift of Mrs. C. J. Martin in memory of Charles Jairus Martin | Minneapolis Institute of Art

This *mille fleurs* (a thousand flowers) style of tapestry, with its profusion of animals and plants, was very popular in the Middle Ages—and remains pleasing today. The animals and foliage are full of vitality. As many as 500 different flowers have been counted.

Large-leaf verdure with birds, ca. 1545–80
Oudenaarde | 9' × 6'1" | Wool, silk | Gift of Mr. and Mrs. Arthur M. Wood, Mrs. Bertha Palmer Thorne, Mrs. Rose Movius Palmer, Mrs. Gordon Palmer | Chicago Art Institute

These leaves create an environment so rich that the viewer might be tempted to dive in. Many animals show up, peeking around the edges.

Greenery

John Henry Dearle, designer | Woven at Merton Tapestry Workshop by John Martin, 1892 | 7' × 15'7" | Wool, mohair | Boston Museum of Fine Arts

In collaboration with Pre-Raphaelite colleagues, and as a way of furthering the British Arts and Crafts movement, William Morris established what became Morris & Co., a furnishings and decorative-arts manufacturer and retailer in England, during the 19th century. Morris taught himself to weave tapestries, which, as he wrote in 1893, was *the noblest of the weaving arts*. In 1881 he founded the Merton Abbey Tapestry Studios.

After Morris's death in 1896, one of his lead designers, John Henry Dearle, continued his work, outliving his mentor by more than 35 years.

The excerpts at the top of the tapestry come from William Morris's writings.

Sarments de Florence I / Vines of Life I
Anet Brusgaard, 1998 | 9'4" × 5'3" | Wool, gold threads, silver threads, silk; cotton warp

The variety of nature formalized in a strict structure

Uccello/Bird
Louis Le Brocquy, designer | Atelier René Duché, 2000 | 5' × 7'6"

A lovely field of leaves, showering down.

Grass
Ildiko Dobranyi | approx. 20" square | Silk, wool

One of a series, each in a different range of colors.

Island Life
Lorna Ramlochansingh, 2000 | 7'6" × 5' | Two-ply wool weft, some handspun, all hand-dyed; cotton seine twine warp | Private collection, Denver, Colorado

Ramlochansingh's roots in the Caribbean have clearly influenced how she treats animals and leaves. The lushness also recalls the 19th-century painter Theodore Rousseau.

Forest Floor
Thoma Ewen, 1998 | 4' × 5' | Wool; cotton warp | Photo: Jamie Cruikshank

Ewen pours in sunlight from above, into a field of greens in a *verdure*.

The Secret Garden
Sharon Marcus, 1985 | 3'11" × 5'9" | Paternayan wool; cotton seine twine warp

A tapestry full of hints and suggestions, where Marcus has broken up the field of green with white, creating positive and negative spaces.

People in Love with Trees
Walter Battiss, South Africa, designer | Stephens Tapestry Studio, Botswana

This piece radiates giddiness. And what exactly will that dog do?

BORDERS, FRAMES

Justicia/Justice
from the series *Los Honores / The Honors* | Designed by Bernard van Orley | Probably from the workshop of Pieter van Aelst, 1520–25 | 17'9" × 14'11" | Wool, silk | Chicago Art Institute

The borders here run along the top and bottom, providing information across the top (in Latin) and developing a complex group of images along the bottom. Van Orley, a famous tapestry designer in the 16th century, conceived of psychologically complex people.

Los Honores consists of nine tapestries, celebrating the election of Charles of Hapsburg as Holy Roman Emperor, 1519.

L'Offrande à Bacchus / Offering to Bacchus

from the series *Les Grotesques* | Designed by Jean-Baptiste Monnoyer and Guy-Louis Vernansal | Beauvais Tapestry Studios, 1688–1732 | 9'8" × 6'8" | Wool, silk | Getty Museum

The borders here are more distinctly frame-like and include a number of grotesques.

The Memorable Judgment of Sancho Panza

from the *Don Quixote* series, #24 of 28 | Designed by Charles Antoine Coypel and others, 1754–58 | Manufacture Nationale des Gobelins | 15'9" × 12'5" | Wool, silk | Metropolitan Museum of Art

Each tapestry in the series about Don Quixote has the same setup, with multiple frames: an episode of the story in the middle, in a frame larger than itself, as though it might be a painting hanging on some highly decorated wallpaper. An outer frame along the edges further surrounds the pastoral scene.

Caribou on the Tundra
Susanne Pretty, 1994 | 41" × 57" | Wool, silk, cotton, linen

In this piece, the TV console functions as a first frame, and the wallpaper, like the ground in *mille fleurs* tapestries, works as an outer frame.

Come on Down!
Meryn Jones | late 1980s

Again, the TV as a frame around the head. The wallpaper provides yet another variation of *mille fleurs*. As Jones would also say, "This is what happens when you watch too much of *The Price is Right*." The woman's feet penetrate the outer frame, and the TV host's mustache adds a suggestive detail.

The Meeting Point
Irina Koleskinova, 2012 | 7.5" × 7.3" | Natural flax, silk; flax warp

The frame is legs and feet. All those shoes point toward a mass of weft irregularly wandering across the warp.

Harmonic Oscillations LXII
James Koehler | Wool

Frames within frames: the cool-blue squares contrast with the more organic inner waves. Koehler was known for his scrupulous attention to color as well as the precision of his weaving.

He taught a small army of students and maintained contact with them, counseling them on their work.

Hills of Grass
Julia Mitchell, 1989 | 38" × 38" | Wool; linen warp

Grass is the subject of Mitchell's tapestry. The center is intentionally blurred, reversing the normal effect of a border.

Between 1986 and 2003, Lilian Tyrrell created a group of 19 huge pieces she called *Disaster Blankets*. In them, she contrasted two characteristics—the appeal of the cloth, a blanket to comfort and warm, and the horror of the subject matter. Thus, the viewer is both attracted and repelled.

#15 Abandoned Heroes
Lilian Tyrrell, 1993 | 7'10" × 10' | Wool, cotton, linen

The bottom of the piece looks like a rug, or a runway, to walk along toward the dead hero. The black verticals frame the hero and hint at a proscenium stage.

#18 Tusks for Trinkets
Lilian Tyrrell, 1999 | 6'10" × 9'8" | Wool, cotton, linen

The slaughtered elephant breaks the gray frame, as its blood pools out along the base.

EMBEDDED IMAGES & IMAGES PURPOSELY OUT OF FOCUS

Mercury Changes Aglauros to Stone, detail
from the series *The Story of Mercury and Herse* | Design attributed to Giovanni Battista Lodi da Cremona, ca. 1540| Studio of Willem Pannemaker, ca. 1570, Belgium | 14'9" × 23'6" (the whole) | Wool, silk, precious metal wrapped threads | Metropolitan Museum of Art

One of eight: the god Mercury takes his **revenge** on Aglauros (*center*), who has tried to keep him from Herse, the object of his **desire**. The figure and the architecture blend into each other.

Palimpsest Series #2
Victor Jacoby | 39" × 38" | Wool

The writing is indecipherable, except, perhaps, for the words *the shadows* (Jacoby made a very large series of tapestries that feature shadow figures). The title is especially apt. The frame almost makes it look like a slide in a mount.

Men in Suits
Andrzej Banachowicz, 2007 | 7'4" × 9'2" | Cotton, sisal, linen, wool

Banachowicz uses line to create his field, to appear and to disappear his figures.

Von Wem ist denn das? / Who Did This?
Peter Horn, 2014 | 7' × 5'3" | Wool

Horn creates a mist around each of the figures. The art on the wall is one of Horn's other tapestries, surveilling the scene.

Waiting
Kay Lawrence, 1998–99 | 4'5" × 5'1" | Wool, cotton; cotton warp

The figure is in haze, like an imprecise recollection.

Conversation at Megido

Barbara Heller, 1988 | 4' × 5'5" | Handspun and commercial wools, all hand-dyed

One of a series in which Heller has explored the histories of stone walls: Who was there? What happened? *Megido* names an important ancient trade route, a narrow pass in northern Israel, said to be where the last battle will be fought. The winner will rule the world. *Megido* is Greek for Armageddon.

Four
TROMPE L'OEIL

Because seeds are like pixels, tapestry weavers can create photorealistic effects—even visual illusions.

In the following pieces, the viewer will be fooled. Most of the tapestries look as though they are dramatically three-dimensional, although each piece lies flat as it hangs on the wall. A hand running along the surface will remain flat.

Gift in Hand
Janet Moore, 1997–98 | 45" × 56" | Wool, raffia; cotton warp | Photo: Cindy Pavlinac

As in the below piece, the shape of the rug is the shape of the tapestry.

The basket and feathers add other textile objects to the whole—and there's also a hand, perhaps clawing its way out.

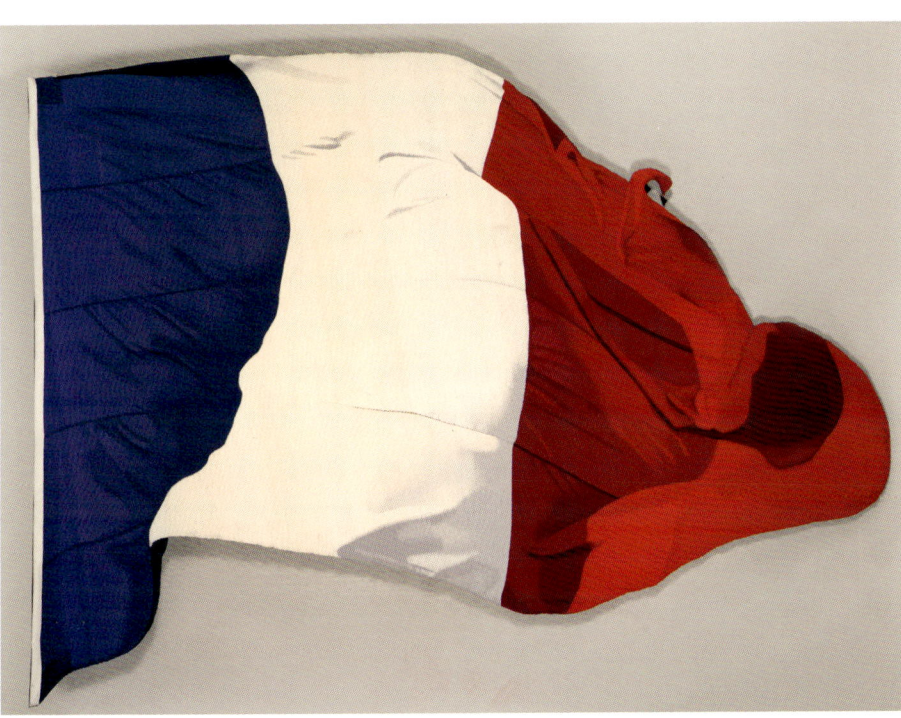

Le drapeau français / The French Flag
Denis Doria, designer | Manufacture Nationale des Gobelins, Paris, France, 1988–92 | Weavers: Marie-Cécile Hauray (team leader), Jean-Pierre Soyer, Agnès Maggiar | 6'6" × 11'6" | Wool | Photo: Françoise Baussan

Woven as part of the national celebrations at the bicentennial of the French Revolution. The shape of the flag is the shape of the tapestry.

Herring Bone Rag
Fiona Mathison, 1974 | 6' × 3'5" | Courtesy of Esta Pekow

Hanging flat on the wall, the tapestry still looks as though the chair awaits the person who wishes to sit. And what should one make of all those trees in areas that are almost windows?

Portal
Elizabeth Buckley, 2005 | 48" × 25" | Wool, cotton, embroidery floss, hand spun, hand-dyed; cotton seine twine warp

Like a curtain waving in the wind against a group of upright poles, confetti flying. Buckley has also, from the center going down, included the illusion of warp.

Drapery Frieze after Leonardo
Lia Cook, 1992 | 4'1" × 5'5" | Acrylic painted on strips of linen interwoven with dyed rayon warp

Inspired by the immense series of drapery drawings by Leonardo da Vinci. The diagonal patterns running through the piece cut the viewer off from the drapery.

Marc Camille Chaimowicz
Elizabeth Radcliffe, 2016 | 59" × 48.4" | Cotton, wool, linen; cotton warp

Marc Camille Chaimowicz and several other woven personages, life size or nearly so, occupy the entry hall to Radcliffe's Edinburgh apartment, disconcerting the unsuspecting visitor. Radcliffe has called attention to her art by treating the face and jacket as though it were a black-and-white photograph, set against the vibrant colors of the chair, the checked pants, and the area rug.

The Other Side of the Curtain
Miyuki Tatsumi, 2011 | 4.7" × 7.5" | Silk

The cityscape is visible amid the folds and drape of the translucent curtain. At this tiny scale, each thread draws the viewer's attention.

Sudden Delight
Inka Kivalo, 2014 | 35.4" × 23.6" | Cotton, silk, linen | Photo: Katja Jagelstam

The shift in tones makes that central rectangle look as though it has lifted straight off the surface and floats.

Broken
Su Egen, 2015 | 46.5" × 26.5" | Swedish wool

Each element—squares that descend, alternating gray and black lines, alternating orange and blue lines—creates another surface that nests inside another surface.

TROMPE L'OEIL

Transformation
David Johnson, 2014 | 45" × 48" | Wool

Everything builds up, as though a child were constructing with bricks or blocks. The butterfly is a surprise. Are those rain clouds in the upper left?

Amaron
Ariadna Donner, 1994 | 12'1" × 8'9" | Wool | Photo: Kaarina Leväniemi

The piece is very large. The bends and folds contrast with the outside, a flat irregular frame.

Emergence I
Rebecca Mezoff, 2009 | 48" × 48" | Hand-dyed wool weft; cotton warp | Photo: Gregory Case

The cloudy white spiral invites a hand to reach through it and touch the red shapes. Mezoff is using bundles of weft threads, with greater or lesser amounts of white, to create that spiral.

Liquid Module I
Tim Gresham, 2007 | 23.6" × 23.6" | Wool, cotton, linen

Such an undulating surface. Which is the object and which is the field?

Esotery
Livia Papai, 1996 | 6' × 6' | Cotton, linen, metallic thread

The title refers to secret wisdom, doubtless somewhere inside this container.

Here Today
Alex Friedman, 2014 | 50" × 35" | Wool; cotton warp

Inspired by a rock formation at the local beach where Friedman had walked for years. She photographed a cliff with a sedimentary chert. She was drawn to the many layers and shadows. She learned it is called ribbon chert. The red seems inspired by the idea of ribbon.

Le Portail / The Portal
Emöke, 2017 | 3'9" × 7'1" | Wool, cotton, linen, raffia, nylon

A very deep perspective: How would one proceed along the pavement to get to the gate? Illusions of paving stones, foliage, roof tiles. The dark center dissipates as the image moves outward.

Certaine Wytches, Chelmsford, England, 1566
Anne Jackson, 2009 | 5'2" × 6'4" | Knotted tapestry—cotton, linen, synthetic yarns | Photo: Mei Lim

Part of a large series about witches. The nooses hanging from rotten frames are especially sinister.

Shadow
Archie Brennan, 1980s | 8" × 8" | Wool; cotton warp

One in a series in which Brennan played with the structures of weaving. Other pieces cover such illusions as *burn, split, slit, stitch*.

Brennan's weaving career spanned more than 70 years; he continues to be regarded as one of the most esteemed and influential tapestry weavers in the world.

The Gordian Knot
Designed by Keith Tyson | Australian Tapestry Workshop, 2017 | Weavers: Sue Batten, Chris Cochius, Pamela Joyce, Milena Paplinska | 7'10.5" in diameter | Wool, cotton

Still on the loom, the warp visible, but the knots and clumps of yarn are vivid. The day-glow colors—and the skill of the weavers—make the tube shapes look reflective, like plastic. Once cut from the loom, the tapestry is round.

Heat Wave
Ann Baddeley Keister, 1988 | 51" × 59" | Wool, silk

Ribbony bands fling themselves about within an architectural structure.

This shaped piece was photographed against a black ground.

Takaro / A Blanket from 1945
Rózsa Polgár

This piece serves as an extremely useful example in showing how deceptive trompe l'oeil can be: the image, the rolled-up fabric, and the faint ripples all occupy the same plane. The mark in the upper right looks as though someone spilled something.

Szövés = Életmód/Weaving = Lifestyle
Judit Nagy, 1980 | 45" × 37"

As though the note had just been torn out of a notebook and pinned to the wall, with texture and wrinkles in the paper. The wallpaper looks like grass cloth. The note itself throws a small shadow.

Foursome Light Blue
Helena Hernmarck, 1989 | 30" × 34" | Wool, linen, cotton

One of many pieces in which Hernmarck plays with folded paper, (sometimes) with watermarks, with embossing.

Hernmarck is renowned for her work with architects, producing tapestries as large as 100 square feet. She seeks to integrate each tapestry into its specific environment.

paper towel
Shelley Socolofsky, 2014 | 5' × 7'5" | Wool, cotton, linen, horsehair, correction fluid

The tapestry is a rectangle, not shaped. Socolofsky wanted to make something mundane into something of immense value. On her breakfast table, she saw the wrinkled paper towel. Odd how the crumpled image can suggest such a collision of forces.

The Three Graces
Andrjez Rajch, 1985 | 8'9" × 6'8" | Wool

About the shifts between black, many grays, and whites. Shapes and folds seem to have volume. Rajch made several such pieces, including at least one in color.

Five
DIRECTIONALITY

In America and Europe, texts read from left to right. In Israel and Arab countries, texts read from right to left. In China, ideograms read from top to bottom, forming columns that are laid down from right to left.

On roads (or bike paths), painters put the beginning of what needs notice first as the car drives, and then the next, and then the next—so the text reads from bottom to top whereas, on the page, it would read from top to bottom.

Just as there are different directions for reading, there are different directions for weaving. A weaver begins at the beginning of the warp and proceeds to weave along its length, interlacing the weft until the work is done. But when the tapestry emerges from the loom, that beginning point becomes either a side, or a bottom, or even a top. That is, some tapestries are hung the way they are woven: the bottom remains the bottom and the top remains the top. In others, the bottom becomes a side.

Noticing the weaver's strategy can provide an extra dimension of interest as you look at a tapestry.

Weavers decide, on the basis of technical and aesthetic priorities, where to begin. They are considering what story they are telling. Beginning at what eventually will be the bottom, the weaver creates a certain image; from the side, another sort of image.

Human figures and European alphabets, for instance, are composed of more vertical elements than horizontal; weaving a horizontal line, which becomes vertical when the tapestry is turned 90 degrees, is simpler than weaving up a warp thread (from bottom to top).

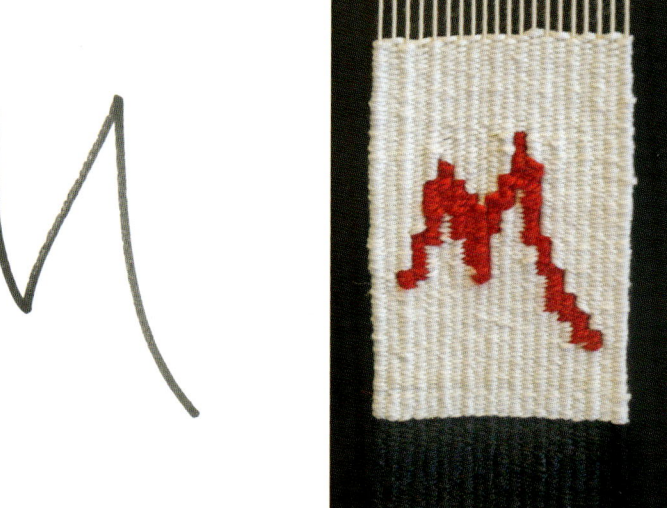

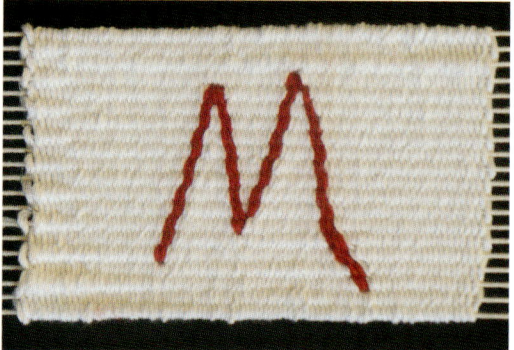

Weaving M

Here, a drawing of a stylized *M*, and two weavings, warp showing:

On the upper right, the *M* is woven from the bottom.

On the lower left, it has been woven from the side.

On the lower right is the same image, turned, so that the bottom becomes the left side of the sampler.

Oilseed Rape Field 1 and 2
Jilly Edwards, 2013 | 4.7" × 3.5" each | Wool, cotton, linen; cotton warp

Edwards's two pieces suggest identical fields at different stages of maturity. She weaves *1* from the bottom and *2* from the side. The slits in the left-hand piece show up as verticals from bottom to top. She has had to weave those areas as lines in the piece on the right. The gray lines in *2* shoot up into the yellow, as a crop would grow.

THE FOLLOWING FIVE TAPESTRIES OFFER CONTENT THAT PROVIDES DIRECTION FOR READING.

Baldisholteppet/Baldishol tapestry, 1150–90
3'10" × 6'8" | Norwegian Museum of Art

This tapestry was woven to follow the order of the year, from left to right, the way Westerners read. Only two months out of twelve remain, almost 900 years after its construction—April (with birds) and May. The names of the months operate like supertitles.

The Apocalypse tapestry, 1377–82
Château of Angers, Loire Valley of France | Photo: © Philippe Berthé/CMN

Based on the biblical book of Revelations, the massive *Apocalypse* tapestry consists of six sections, each approximately 20' × 78', and follows the course of the narrative. Each section alternates the color of the ground in the individual episodes—red or blue.

The tapestry tells the tale in sequence, like a comic strip, bit by bit. In the château, the tapestry hangs along a corridor that traces the external curves of the building, above the heads of the visitors. Saint John, on the left of each panel, witnesses this vision of the end of the world, all the astonishing beasts and tales of horror and possibility.

The bottom of the tapestry, as woven, became the left side.

What happens if a tapestry of such immense size as the *Apocalypse* is woven from the bottom as it hangs?

At minimum, two problems:

First, the sheer weight of weft will press downward along the warp, compressing and distorting the images. Second, warp wound onto a loom beam can be far longer than the width of the loom. If these 78-foot lengths measured no more than 20 feet, the nature and feeling of the vast piece would change radically.

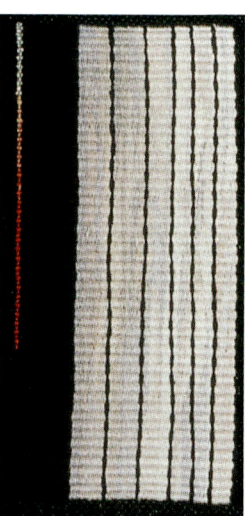

Never Again

individual pieces (from left to right): ***Beginnings, Kristalnacht, Badges, Incarceration, Final Journey, Finale***

Renate Chernoff, 1998 | 6" × 4" each | Cotton embroidery yarn, wool

This series of small pieces forms a clear narrative, leaving only a sliver of possibility at the end. The individual tapestries need one another to tell the whole story.

Black + White + Red All Over #18: The alphabet
Micala Sidore, 1999 | 4.5" × 6' | Cotton

Here the left-to-right progression occurs in a single tapestry. The entire series *Black + White + Red All Over* consists of over 60 pieces, each of which is made up of pieces woven only with black, white, and red. This tapestry runs through the alphabet, with red inserted where it belongs.

Crayola
Lialia Kuchma, 1982 | 4' × 11' | Wool; cotton warp

In this piece, color and tone progress, the eye moving from left to right, from the paler gray ground to the darker. The details, all those lines both straight and slightly curved, grow insistently brighter and perhaps even take on greater definition, as the ground around them grows darker.

This tapestry prompted me to follow the idea of directionality as a way to see tapestries.

WEAVING TIME

In each of the following tapestries, the weaver begins by inserting the yarn at the bottom and proceeding to the top. The first three, calendars, record the passing of time in a year as the weaver proceeds along the warp. Several contemporary weavers create annual tapestry diaries, reflecting on each day, each week, each month, each season. A fourth tapestry records not only time passing, but also changes in the life of the weaver.

Into the Hills
Janette Meetze, 2015 | 32" × 40.5" | Wool, silk, cotton; cotton warp | Photo: Janette Meetze

While each individual shape, defined by color and pattern, indicates another day, one can appreciate how Meetze also tells the viewer about the colors of her Oklahoma home.

Above: *Tapestry Diary, 2016*
Tommye Scanlin, 2016 | 54" × 14" × 2" | Wool; linen warp, black walnut and commercial dyes

Scanlin raids her Georgia garden to obtain the dyestuffs she uses. Black walnut is a favorite. Here, she weaves larger plants set up like photographs on a page to mark months, with framing stripes to count the days.

Left: *2015 Tapestry Diary*
Janet Austin, 2015 | 45" × 12" | Wool, cotton, linen, silk | Photo: Jan Austin

Austin chose a particular color scheme or technique for each month.

The Journey Back
Linda Wallace, 2013–15 | 44" × 33" × 1" | Wool, cotton, linen, silk; cotton warp

After Wallace suffered a stroke, she was determined to continue her weaving. Friends helped her warp the loom. Over the next two years, bit by bit, she wove, from the bottom to the top: small, simple geometric shapes; more-intentional checkerboards; and, finally, a flowering, a wild, free association of line and space, as though she could now celebrate what she had regained.

Above: *Sequencing Time*
Joan Griffin, 2014 | 38" × 12" | Wool; cotton warp

A tapestry about geology, the ways that the earth forms, layer by layer, from deep down, red magma, to the blue of the sky. A far deeper measure of time.

Left: *Aphorism Kilim*
Kay Lawrence, 1987–91 | 8'4" × 2'9" | Wool, cotton, linen; cotton warp

Along **three** sides, Lawrence quotes a useful statement from Archie **Brennan**: *Tapestry is like life—you can't undo what you did yesterday, but you can modify it by what you do today.* Triangles break the frame and so emphasize **the** words.

WEAVING SPACE

Home, Away
Joy Smith, 2004 | 4" × 6" (each) | Wool; cotton warp

Smith, an Australian, was at an artist residency in England. The colors around her were dramatically other than what she was accustomed to. Australia is known for its red center. The sheep are a constant.

En France II
Cresside Collette, 2013 | 8.7" × 3.1" | Wool, cotton, synthetic; cotton warp

The eye moves as it studies the whole of the landscape, from bottom to top, along the road, the forest, the line of trees and shadows, the hills, the sky and clouds. The weaver starts with the nearest element of the landscape, progressing to the most distant.

Menai Last Light
Ros Hornbuckle, 2018 | 23.6" × 35.4" | Wool; cotton warp

Bodies of water interact with the sky above, a slender line between them.

Footprints & Horizon
Soon Yul Kang, 2014 | 5.9" × 20.1" | Wool, cotton

Slowly, deliberately, as they would in sand, the footprints appear, one after the other, just as the weaver proceeds, from bottom to top. Slowly the ocean spreads across the width, and then the constant of the horizon line.

Canyon Dusk
Pat Dozier, 2015 | 59" × 15" | Wool

The horizon cuts the image neatly in half; the sky and the canyon colors reflect back on each other.

The Road to Haleakala
Susan Martin Maffei, 1991 | 53" × 17" | Wool, cotton, linen; cotton warp

Haleakala, an East Maui volcano in Hawaii, means *the house of the sun*. The road begins at the bottom, at a sign that specifies where it goes.

The weaver begins at this sign. The action of weaving echoes the way that the road moves, from left to right and back again.

Field Blowing
Julia Mitchell, 1981 | 45" × 45" | Wool; linen warp

The swing in weaving back and forth lends itself easily to rendering of the grasses, which look bent over because of wind. In addition, Mitchell has constructed a frame, as though she could somehow contain the force of what blows.

WEAVING ABSTRACTIONS

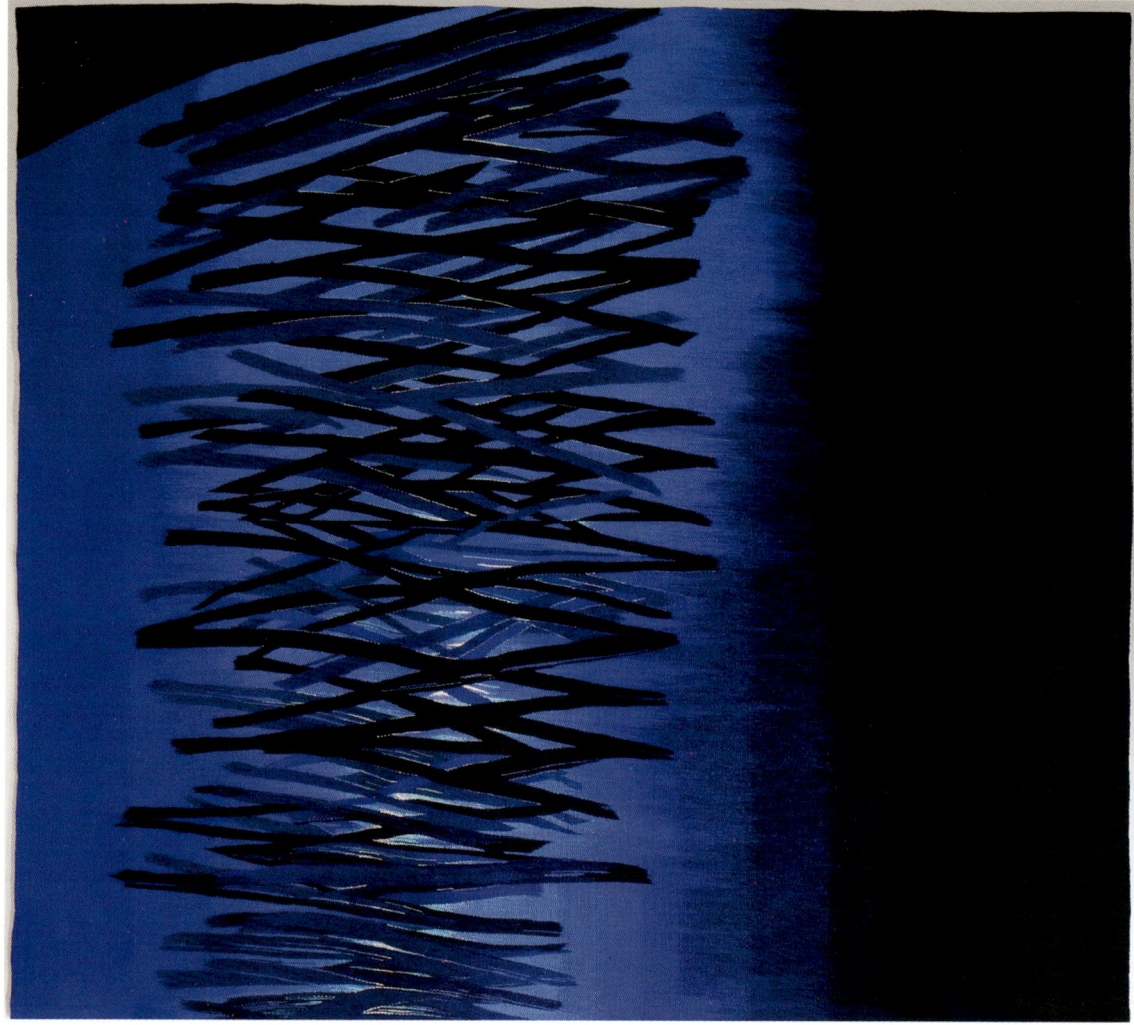

Blue
Lialia Kuchma, 2003 | 5'10" × 5'10" | Wool; cotton warp

The energy here shivers. On the left, lines like wicker vibrate against the still darkness of the right.

Imaginary Landscape II
Betsy Wing, 2010 | 34" × 23" | Wool; cotton warp | Photo: Lawrence Matson

A weaver would see immediately that Wing wove this tapestry from the bottom. Certain narrow lines—the peachy orange that defines the waves of blues—cannot be woven until the blues are complete. The sense of discovery—the *oh!*—is very strong.

Partial Sunlight
Rachel Brown, 1990 | 5' × 3'4" | Hand-dyed wool

In this piece, the tones carry the eye, from bottom left to top right, from dark to light.

For years, Brown taught classes; ran a gallery in Taos that showed contemporary work of New Mexico makers; wrote a major book on weaving, spinning, and dyeing; and inspired generations.

Quiet Playground
Susan Edmunds, 2009 | 34.5" × 39.5" | Wool; linen warp

The tapestry has the look of a manuscript, something to be read and savored.

Homecoming Kings
Julia Rapinoe, 2012 | 7" × 6" | Silk; linen warp

The herringbone pattern looks like arrows pointing and might just have a shimmer from its material: silk threads. The energy moves back and forth.

The herringbones in red also suggest the salmon, wriggling their way home.

Jazz
Judith Poxson Fawkes, 2001 | 3'5" × 5'4" | Linen double weave

The piece works in beats like the imagined music. Diagonals play against strong verticals. Fawkes employed complex weaving patterns in her work.

The Traveller
Valerie Kirk, 2017 | 56" × 29.5" | Wool; cotton seine twine warp

What looks like fringe, or stitches, embeds the image of the figure in its environment.

DIRECTIONALITY

Blue Bleak Embers

Mary Rawcliffe Colton, 1982 | 5'1" × 2'4" | Wool; linen warp

The title comes from a line in *The Windhover* by Gerard Manley Hopkins.

The eye looks for a place to begin to look. From the bottom, the shape rises and narrows, from light to dark.

Balancing Act

Donna Martin, 1995 | 59.5" × 24.5" | Wool, mohair; vegetal dyes

Shapes like books piled high.

WOVEN FROM THE SIDE

How do weavers orient themselves to the designs they interpret?

They learn.

At la Manufacture Nationale des Gobelins in Paris, weavers work from the backside of the tapestry. Now and then, they separate the vertical parallel lines of warp, with thumb and forefinger, to look at a mirror, which shows them what is completed on the front.

During the 1980s, a team began a tapestry from the top of the design. They had determined that it was strategically sensible to begin it there.

Weavers learn to shift their attention easily between the detail and the whole.

this takes time
Ruth Manning, 2003 | 12" × 14" (including the trailing yarn) | Wool, cotton

Sometimes, attention frays as the weaver works.

Cadence
Marta Rogoyska, 2016 | 14" × 13" | Hand-dyed wool; cotton warp

Each small detail, each small irregularity, in the shape of each stripe, or its edges, or its dominant color, shows the weaver's decision-making. No drips of paint here—Rogoyska is advertising the fact that she is weaving.

Reflets/ Reflections
Marie-Thumette Brichard, 2007 | 4'9.5" × 6'3.5" | Wool

The cool blues suggest meditation, as the weaver composes these irregular stripes.

Etude #6, Change
Joyce Hayes, 2013 | 12" × 12.5" × 1.5" (tapestry is 5.75" × 6.25") | Naturally dyed silk thread, *soumak*, rayon thread | The maroon base is steel; linen warp

Faint horizontal lines, like ribs, indicate structure, where the weft is concealing warp.

DIRECTIONALITY

131

Echo
Unn Sonju, 1982–83 | 1'4" × 65'6" | Wool; linen warp

Sonju finishes both sides of her piece so that one can read either. She uses short poles as a device to help it run along walls and turn corners. The images read from left to right, from light to dark, telling an ongoing story.

Image of a Growing Spring
Ulrika Leander, 1995 | 2'1" × 12'6" | Wool; cotton warp

Time passes in this tapestry, as flowers grow over time, different flowers as the spring deepens.

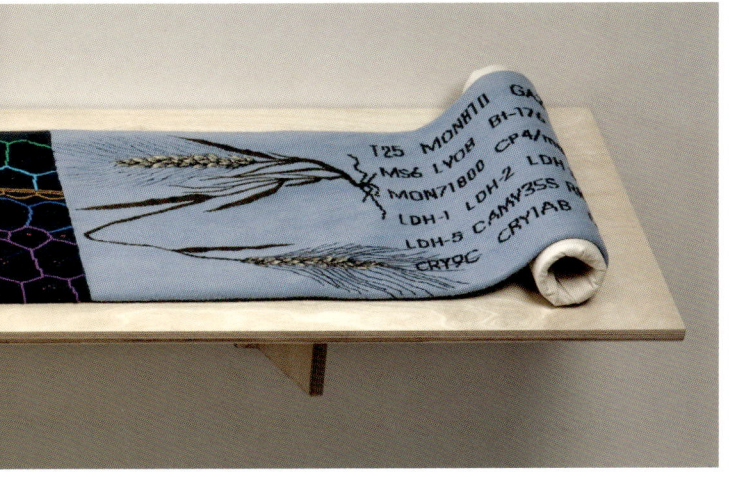

Wonderland series: curiouser and curiouser #1
Jane Kidd, 2015 | 1'6" × 8'2" | Wool, cotton, rayon

Kidd made several pieces as she considered *Alice in Wonderland*. Color defines the sections here. The bowl almost looks as though it is floating above its place in the scroll.

Too Much Sand / Soooo Good
Amanda Gizzi, 2014 | 7.9" × 6" | Cotton, linen

In a shower, the water falls as though from an angle on the left, where the weaver began, soaking the body.

Six
TEXTILES AND IDENTITIES, WHEN TEXTILES DEFINE A PARTICULAR GROUP

Groups in certain regions of the world identify themselves through their textiles. The look and the work of the cloth help define who their members are, what history they share, what matters.

Some of these societies trace their textile roots back millennia.

Some textiles make for a visual language, a nonalphabetic means of communication.

KILIMS, DHURRIES

Kilims are flat-woven rugs, a kind of tapestry found in West and South Asia and in eastern Europe (dhurries are the rough equivalent in India). Most of what we see here shows contemporary weavers reworking earlier traditions.

Prayer Kilim, 1875–1900
3'4" × 6'3" | Wool | Gift of Richard L. and Roberta G. Simmons | Minneapolis Institute of Art

All one piece, woven in five distinct sections, each one varying certain basic elements.

Two Contemporary Kilims (details)
Konya, Turkey, 2013 | The wholes: 55" × 38", 51" × 42"

Aydin Nomad
Musa Basaran, 2009 | 51" × 38" | Silk, natural dyes

Ram's Horn
Musa Basaran, 2016 | 3'11" × 5'11" | Silk, natural dyes

This kilim and the kilim on the previous page are satisfying and complex contemporary pieces. Hints of traditional kilim designs abound. All those interlocking shapes.

The rest of the images in this chapter come from the Western Hemisphere.

SALISH

Weavers of the Pacific Northwest. Known for their twill blankets, they bred a woolly dog in order to have its fur to incorporate into their weavings (the dog went extinct by 1875).

Salish tapestry, before 1828
44.5" × 59.4" | Mountain goat, woolly dog | National Museum of Finland | Photo: Markku Haverinen

Standing Together—Our Culture, Our Strength
Christine Rivers, 2015 | outer pieces—11.5" × 15.5", center piece—12" × 16" | Wool, silk, wool blend, feathers and beads sewn on, copper-colored metallic; cotton warp

Small pieces to be hung on the wall.

SOUTHWESTERN NORTH AMERICA

Where the traditions of tapestry weaving are among the most ancient found in North America.

NAVAJO

From a group of samplers:
Left: Lynda Teller Pete | Classic serape design | 16.5" × 12.5"
Right: Navajo dress design | 12.5" × 10.5" | Photos: Belvin Pete

Teller Pete belongs to the fifth generation of a family long renowned for their weavings in the Two Grey Hills style. She wove these small pieces, two of about a dozen, illustrating specific textile traditions—a serape, a Navajo dress. The pieces contain political meaning. The title of the serape (left), *Arrowheads for Strength*, comes from the tradition of including arrowheads to prepare for something frightening up ahead. The dress called *Hope* (right) includes four lines at the bodice, to encourage the wearers to believe that they will return to their four sacred mountains. In recent years, the tendency to identify such weavings as *Navajo* or by its *style* is yielding to the practice of naming the individual weavers.

Baa'Hózhó
D. Y. Begay, 2014 | 25.5" × 41" | Wool, homegrown churro and karakul (breeds of sheep)

The title is a Navajo word and the basis for Navajo thought. Begay says, "The Navajo believe the world to be an orderly place filled with interconnected objects all existing in a state of balance and harmony.

"The foundation of my religion is Hózhó; to me it means being in a state of completeness, balance, harmony and contentment." The stripes here balance without symmetry.

Blessings of Rain
D. Y. Begay, 2015 | 26" × 46" | Churro, karakul, merino

Rain brings life.

Axis Radius
Marlowe Katoney, 2016 | 36" × 24" | Wool

Katoney inserts his own eye into traditional Navajo imagery.

HOPI

Eclipse I
Ramona Sakiestewa, 2006 |
24.4" × 25"

Sakiestewa has included elements such as windows, like shards, almost like mirrors.

Urban Galaxy 4
Ramona Sakiestewa, 2006 |
46" × 46"

TEXTILES AND IDENTITIES

SALTILLO

Saltillo Serape, 1800–50
7'8.5" × 3'6" | Cotton, wool, cochineal and other dyes | Heard Museum, Phoenix, Arizona | Photo: Craig Smith

This style of weaving begins during the 1500s and originated in the city of Saltillo, Mexico; a tradition of handwoven blankets worn by the Aztecs. The weavings feature diamond shapes in the center and are often woven as two pieces and then joined together.

CHIMAYO, NEW MEXICO

Grace
Irvin Trujillo, 2010 | 7' × 4'8" | Natural dyes, mill-spun wool

Trujillo is a seventh-generation Rio Grande weaver, a tradition dating from the mid-16th century. He pursues the established practices as well as his own vision. These include rectangular-shaped weaving, central image, stripes, and frames. He works while standing at a horizontal warp loom.

In 2007 the NEA declared him a National Heritage Fellow.

Four Season Tree
Lisa Trujillo, 2008 | 7' × 4'8" | Natural dyes, mill-spun wool

Lisa Trujillo learned to weave after her marriage to Irvin, and together they run the studio known as Chimayo Weavers, in New Mexico.

Passion in the Web
Lisa Trujillo, 2015 | 7'4" × 4'10" | Natural dyes, mill-spun wool

A festival of diamonds

ZAPOTEC, OAXACA, MEXICO

An indigenous population of Mexico, already well established before the Spanish conquest. Known for their weaving, Zapotecs have made famous the village of Teotitlán del Valle, Oaxaca. Several Zapotec weavers also live in the United States and Canada.

Huipil de las Ideas
Luis Lazo, 2013 | 17.25" × 13" | Wool, silk; cotton warp

A *huipil* is a garment worn throughout Central America. The tapestry shows a richly elaborated field, where there is a hint of the neck hole (*at the top left*).

Celestial Space
Porfirio Gutierrez, 2015 | 47.2" × 35.4" | Wool; natural dyes: indigo, cochineal, tree moss, tarragon

The lack of symmetry works to highlight opposing colors and patterns.

Maíz Plant
Porfirio Gutierrez, 2017 | 6'6" × 4'3" | Natural sheep color wool; natural dyes: cochineal, tree moss, marigold, zapote negro (a type of persimmon), indigo

Like a field of corn that grows from bottom to top, from early in the season to full maturity.

El Jaguar
Francisco Ruiz Martinez, 2014 | 37" × 34" | Wool, gold, silver; cotton warp

That jaguar wears a pretty spectacular headdress.

Quetzalcoatl, la Serpiente Emplumada / The Plumed Serpent
Francisco Ruiz Martinez, 2018 | 31.5" × 27.5" | Wool, natural dyes

A god whom the Aztecs turned into a symbol of death and rebirth.

Buffalo Robe Red
Wence Martinez, 2016 | 5'2" × 3'3" | Wool

Elegant and satisfying.

Floating Hawks
Wence and Sandra Martinez, 2008 | 9' × 9'4" | Wool

The couple, who have collaborated for over 30 years, live in her native Wisconsin. Her imagery connects with his Zapotec traditions. Here the repeated motif in the central panel seems like a fence through which one looks.

Aires Zapotecos / Zapotec Airs
Erasto (Tito) Ruiz Mendoza, 2011 | 47.2" × 39.4" | Cotton, silk, wool

Two contrasting styles—one geometric and one representational.

Arropame / Wrap Me Up
Erasto (Tito) Ruiz Mendoza, 2013 | 37" × 35" | Silk, wool, gold and silver details; cotton warp

Again, contrasting styles—a *saltillo*-like central diamond, shawl segments that hang from opposing corners, footprints, cartoon bits, a profile of someone looking into the distance.

Cosijo
Jacobo Mendoza, 2016 | 23.6" × 19.7" | Silk, wool; cotton warp

Also referred to as *Cocijo*—Zapotec god of rain and lightning.

Guerrero Ocho Venado / Warrior Eight Deer
Jacobo Mendoza, 2010 | 43.3" × 29.5" | Silk, silk thread bathed in gold

A detail in the founding story from Mixtec myths.

Mendoza is one of ten brothers and sisters, all of whom weave (even the lawyer).

Laberinto Constelado / Concentrated Labyrinth
Maria Luisa Vásquez de Mendoza, 2012 | 19.7" × 23.6" | Merino, baby alpaca, silk

Sky above. A path that works its way up. Around the path, friezes about the cycle of life.

Caballo Artistico / Artistic Horse
Maria Luisa Vásquez de Mendoza, 2014 | 20" × 19" | Wool, silk

The slight blur around its legs makes the horse look as though it sways or even prances over a rigidly geometric design.

Caracol/Snail
Pedro Mendoza Gutierrez

The repeated curling motif comes from designs at archeological sites in Oaxaca. Familial traditions say that it signifies life cycles.

Mazorca Hispanica / Prehispanic Ear of Corn
Rufina Mendoza, 2014 | 23.6" × 15" | Silk, wool, gold thread, vegetal dyes; cotton warp

WESTERN SOUTH AMERICA

Geographically, the following group of pieces comes from a large swath of land, centered in the Andes Mountains, much of which, from the fourteenth to the sixteenth centuries, included the Inca Empire. This area includes several distinct cultural groups.

OTAVALO, ECUADOR

Otavalo tapestry detail, 1970s | 38" × 30.5" | Wool

The Otavalo are known for their international travels, where they market what they produce and perform Andean music on traditional instruments. Also for the tweed-like color combinations in their weavings—the darker birds in this Escher-like piece.

SALASACA, ECUADOR

A regional textile museum is located in the heart of the town.

Two Figures
Curi Antonio Masaquiza Caisabanda, 2016

El Danzante / The Dancer
Curi Antonio Masaquiza Caisabanda, 2016
| 51.6" × 19.7"

PERU

The next four weavers trace their roots to the Wari, who flourished in the south-central Andes and coastal area of modern-day Peru from about the years 500 to 1000 CE. The Wari produced beautiful weavings and developed the knotting system known as *quipu*, which served to keep track of populations and agricultural production. (The Inca developed *quipu* further.)

Camino Ardiente de la Luz / Burning Road of Light
Maximo Laura, 2007 | 4' × 7'8" | Cotton, alpaca, mixed fibers

Peru and UNESCO have named Laura a Living National Treasure. His brilliantly colored tapestries tell the ancestral myths in which opposites play a major role.

He has a studio in Callao (next to Lima), a gallery in Cuzco, and returns regularly to his native Ayacucho. He considers himself part of a lost generation, many of whom died during the period of *Sendero Luminoso* / Shining Path, which terrorized his home region during the 1980s and early 1990s.

Fiesta de la Diosa del Agua / Festival of the Water Goddess
Maximo Laura, 2005 | 4' × 15'4" | Cotton, alpaca, mixed fiber

AYACUCHO, PERU

Domingo de Ramos / Palm Sunday
Cyprian Fernandez, 2016 | 5'3" × 4' | Sheep's wool

Palm Sunday, the first Sunday of Holy Week, is a festival day in Ayacucho and includes Christ entering the city on a burro. People are holding palms in their hands, showing both happiness and pride.

Awaq Uru / Weaving Spider
Cyprian Fernandez, 2016 | 5'3" × 4' | Sheep's wool

The spider, a weaver, is iconography found in Peruvian textiles. Generally, this imagery appears often during the period of the Wari.

Angeles Wari / Wari Angels
Alexander Gallardo, 2016 | 47.2" × 35.4" | Alpaca

This is inspired by Wari clothing called *unku* (meaning "tunic"), based on actual historical weavings.

As well as his work as a weaver, following in his father's footsteps, Gallardo is an archeologist.

Tapiz Wari / Wari Rug
Alexander Gallardo, 2016 | 47.2" × 35.4" | Alpaca

The artistic style of the tapestry belongs to the second stage of cultural development among the Wari.

A woven band?
Alfonsin Sulca, 2016

In Ayacucho, capital of the Peruvian state of the same name, an office on the main square displays huge photographs of valued local makers. Sulca and Maximo Laura are the two tapestry weavers. Sulca is known for images of three-dimensional bands—which look here like a roll of film.

A pilgrimage?
Alphonsin Sulca, 2016

Perhaps the story of a pilgrimage, following a specific pathway, each individual with offerings.

INCA/QUECHUA

Half Tunic, *16th century*
Peru, south coast | Inca culture, colonial period | 37.5" × 28.5" | Cotton, wool | Cleveland Museum of Art

A hybrid of Inca and Spanish colonial culture. The Spanish influence appears in the open sides of the garment, the animals in the yoke, as well as the flowers.

CHECACUPE, PERU

Los Cuatro Suyos / The Four Regions
Gabina Ccallo Quispe, 2016 | 32" × 30" | Alpaca

The geometric shapes work from traditional models, four districts visible in the colors and variety of patterns. Originates with the organization of the Incan Empire.

CHINCHERO, PERU

Two figures
Angel Ligorio Callañaupa, 2016 | Alpaca, llama and sheep's wool; natural dyes

Callañaupa's tapestries rework Inca textile *qompi*, also known as the discontinuous style. The images play with the Andean vision of the cosmos.

Callañaupa is an illustrator of children's books as well as a weaver.

PITUMARCA, PERU

Timoteo Sacaca Ccarita, 2016

Timoteo Sacaca Ccarita, 2016

Each of the tapestries tells another of the local myths that Sacaca grew up with, framed by a geometric border.

In Sucre, one of Bolivia's two capitals, ASUR (Antropólogos del Surandino / Anthropologists of the Southern Andes) is an organization that seeks to help local communities maintain and strengthen their cultural identity and economic conditions by promoting the production and sale of high-quality indigenous arts, such as textiles.

TARABUCO, BOLIVIA

Tarabuco, 2000 | Bolivia | Detail (The whole is 31" × 33".)

The design is highly organized, in lines, with repeated images, full of brilliant color and recognizable people and animals.

JALQ'A

Jalq'a, 2000 | Detail (The whole is 36" × 30".) | Traditional double cloth

The landscape is that of *ukhu pacha*, a sacred world including a somewhat chaotic assemblage of fantastic beasts and figures. The other side shows the reverse: black figures in a red field.

Child's tapestry, 2016 | 18" × 11.25"

Among the Jalq'a, ASUR has provided lessons in more-traditional tapestry techniques to adults and children. Like in their black-and-red double weaves, the results crowd many people and beasts into a formal frame.

The following three tapestries—from Peru, New Mexico, and Mexico—suggest a broader context, an awareness of the world of the weaver, and how each weaver understands tradition.

PERU

Tuñel del Tiempo / The Tunnel of Time
Alejandro Gallardo, 2016 | 29.6" × 23.1" | Alpaca

Woven by the father of Alexander Gallardo, the piece includes visual reference to five Andean cultures: Chavin, Paracas, Wari, Chimu, and Inca.

NEW MEXICO

Profile
Irvin Trujillo, 2013 | 6' × 4' | Mill-spun wool, natural dyes

According to Trujillo, the three profiles show how he and his wife look at each other, and his father, behind, watches both of them.

MEXICO

Laba xte ladi nuy / Raíces del tapiz / Roots of Tapestry
Marcelina Mendoza, 2014 | 20.7" × 12.6" | Silk, wool, gold thread, vegetal dyes; cotton warp

The words of the first title are in Zapotec. Mendoza has situated her work deep in the local environment.

Seven
SELF-REFERENCE

This section includes weavers who refer to cloth directly by picturing it—especially as clothing and furnishings. Some copy particular objects with scrupulous exactness, such as an upholstered chair woven with the fiber used for the actual piece of furniture. Or they abstract a pattern from the represented object. Some see an exciting technical challenge in rendering the drape of clothing or furnishings—even the idiosyncrasies of skin and hair. They weave images of folds that create illusions of dimensionality.

Histoire du Roi: Le roi visitant les Gobelins le 15 octobre 1667 / The History of the King: The King Visiting les Gobelins, 15 October 1667

Designed by Charles le Brun, 1690 | Atelier de Jans fils | 16'8" × 23' | Wool, silk, golden thread

In 1662, French King Louis XIV (through his finance minister Jean-Baptist Colbert) united a variety of independent studios into La manufacture royale des meubles de la couronne (the Royal Manufacture of the Crown's Furniture). Early on, the weavers, under the direction of Charles le Brun, wove a series of 14 tapestries, devoted to the life of the king, L'Histoire du Roi. They made a particularly canny choice with this piece, which celebrates the weavers as well as their patron.

Cloth is everywhere here. *At the left*, one sees the king, with a red plume in his chapeau, amid his courtiers, all dressed in magnificent clothing and wearing elaborate wigs. In front of them, workers are rolling up at least one tapestry and a rug. Other workers wrestle with furniture, which the studio also produced.

At the right, a curtain hangs. Centrally placed, something looking like a completed tapestry (of a battle) hangs—it is actually a cartoon, a design for a future date, part of a series about Alexander the Great.

The Otter and the Swan, detail
From *The Devonshire Hunting Tapestries* | 10'8" × 28'4" (the whole) | Wool | © Victoria and Albert Museum, London

The Devonshire tapestries comprise a suite of four pieces from the mid-15th century. The range of details in the clothing, the illusion of the dimensions of the human body, have inspired present-day makers. That said, such restricting and exotic clothes are undoubtedly *not* what actual hunters would have worn.

On the left side of this detail, adjacent to two women, stand two men in turbans. Dots of various sizes and density help define the shapes of their bodies.

Woman in a Spotted Dress / At a Window 1
Archie Brennan, designer, 1972 | Dovecot Tapestry Studio, 1978 | 7' × 5' | Wool, cotton

The first in Brennan's immense series of tapestries titled *At a Window*. The designs in the framing curtains contrast with the woman in her dress. The details show how, very deliberately, the weaver has used individual dots to evoke the contours of the body.

The Arming of the King
Designed by Bernard Partridge; borders designed by John Henry Dearle, 1912–14 | 10'9" × 14'3" | Wool, silk | Boston Museum of Fine Arts

All that material, including metal armor and animal skin. The four women represent allegorical figures who endow the king with the qualities he needs to rule. Depending on how one sees the tapestry, it has at least two subjects: rule— and clothing.

Imperial Court robe, 17th century
Qing dynasty | 6'2" × 4'8" | Silk, metallic thread | Metropolitan Museum of Art

The Chinese tradition of tapestries, known as *kesi* or *k'ossu* (both words mean "cut silk"), appears in elaborate designs on their robes and other garments.

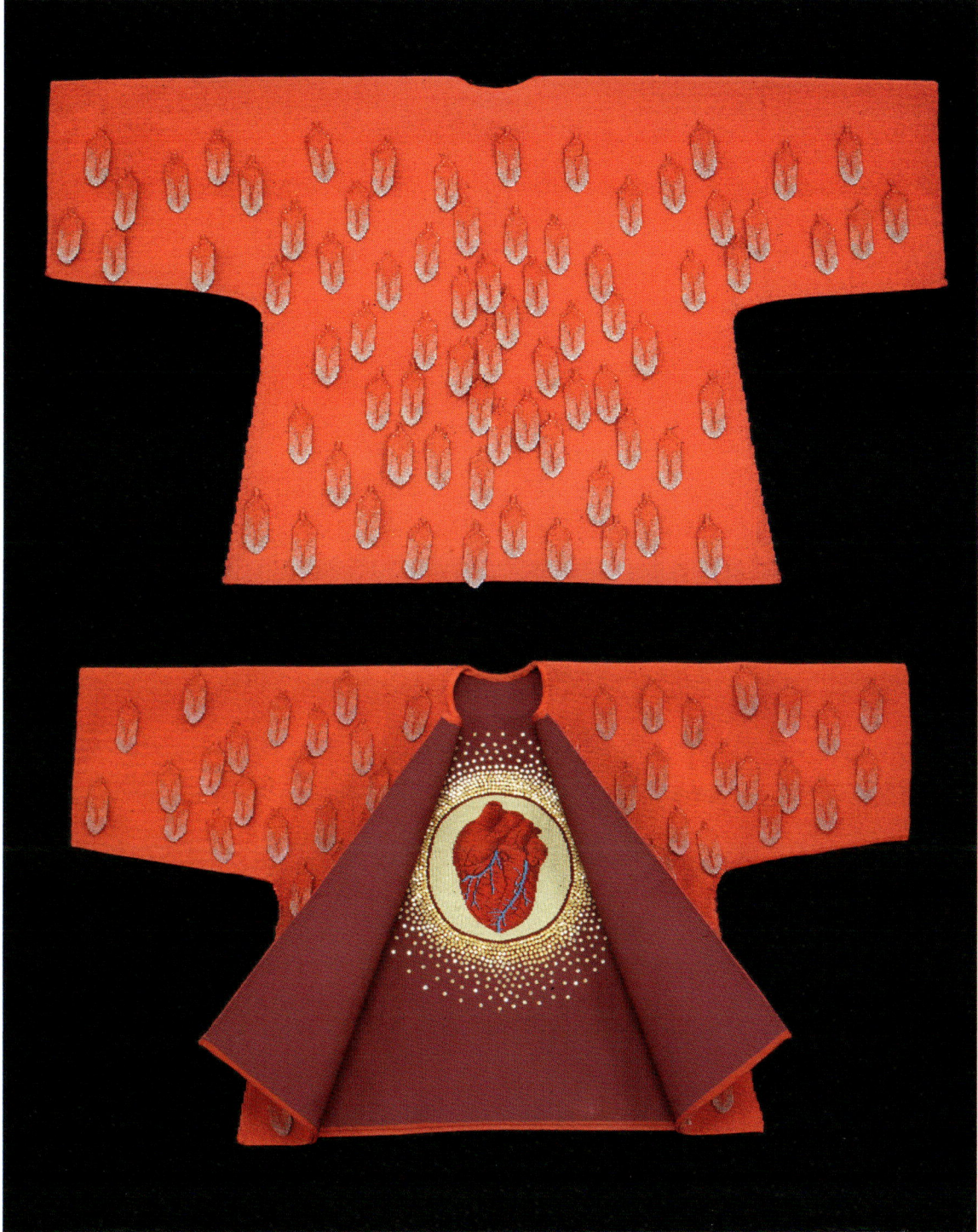

Cardinal's Coat, outside and inside
Jon Eric Riis, 2007 | 22" × 42" | Silk, metallic thread

The shape of the garment is the shape of the tapestry. The coat can be put on and worn: one of Riis's approximately three dozen woven coats. Each tells a particular tale, of a culture, a political moment, an origin. Riis is, among other things, an expert in Asian textiles.

A Coat for Mother Earth
Anita Berman, 1989 | Rayon, paint

Berman's ecological concerns led her to weave a coat for the fragile world.

Rayon gives the coat sheen—but the ragged-looking painted warps suggest unease about the present.

It's just so hard to decide what to wear
Sarah Swett, 1998 | 36" × 48" | Wool

In Swett's very funny tapestry, there are echoes of the iconic poster from the Brooklyn Museum Art School in which a group of naked students in front of easels draw a clothed model. These clothes have a life of their own.

Sisters in Hats
Martha Matthews, 1983 | 43" × 50" | Wool, linen, cotton

Matthews took care to use materials, such as linen for the hat on the sister to the left, to replicate every detail of what they wore.

Grace
Kathy Spoering, 2012 | 10" × 8" | Wool; cotton warp

Of all the textile allusions in this piece—the sweater, the hair, the kitten's fur, the nest—only one is not fiber: the actual metal tag hanging from the kitten's collar.

Amish Boy
Bonnie Platzer, 2017 | 40.5" × 34.75" | Paternayan wool; cotton warp

Platzer has traveled extensively, but her work, while including the foreign landscape, also shows how people live their everyday lives. The boy is entirely intent on the bandanas he is hanging. Other textile elements include the straw hat, his bangs, and the clothesline. Behind, the landscape provides a patterned contrast.

Ketao Market
Bonnie Platzer, 2000 | 46" × 58" | Paternayan wool; cotton warp

A piece about stripes—and about the bodies inside. Ketao is in Togo.

A Fine Thread
Lise DeCoursin, 2003 | 20" × 20" | Wool; cotton warp

The stance of the woman recalls medieval tapestry, as do the clothing, the head scarf, and the thread being spun, trailing off the bottom of the piece.

Four Girls and an Apple, Mustang, Nepal
Eve Pearce, 1999 | 48" × 50" | Wool, cotton; cotton warp | Photo: Art Evans

Pearce has constructed a range of textures here, such as the fur edging worn by the girl on the far left, the shoes, the bag held by the girl on the far right, the apple.

Hartland Map series, *Phantom Ranch, Crossroads*
Susan Hart Henegar, 2008 | 36" × 36" (× 2) | Wool

Historically, maps might be printed on cloth. Henegar has made eight parts for this group, showing an identifiable southwestern United States. When fully installed, each piece remains distinct from the others, as though separated by the folds of a paper road map. Some of the sections are quilted; these two are woven.

Siete Marias / Seven Marias
Andrea Milde, 1997–2001 | approx. 5'3" × 14'9" | Cotton, gold Lurex, linen, silk, wool; undyed wool warp

These seven women, in their head scarves, shawls, aprons, and skirts, resemble each other—and yet remain highly individual. There is something familiar, in many cultures, about women sitting together outside, talking.

Stamps
Tricia Goldberg, 2004 | 38" × 49" | Wool, silk; cotton warp

Handsomely and hugely enlarged from an envelope from a friend in Japan.

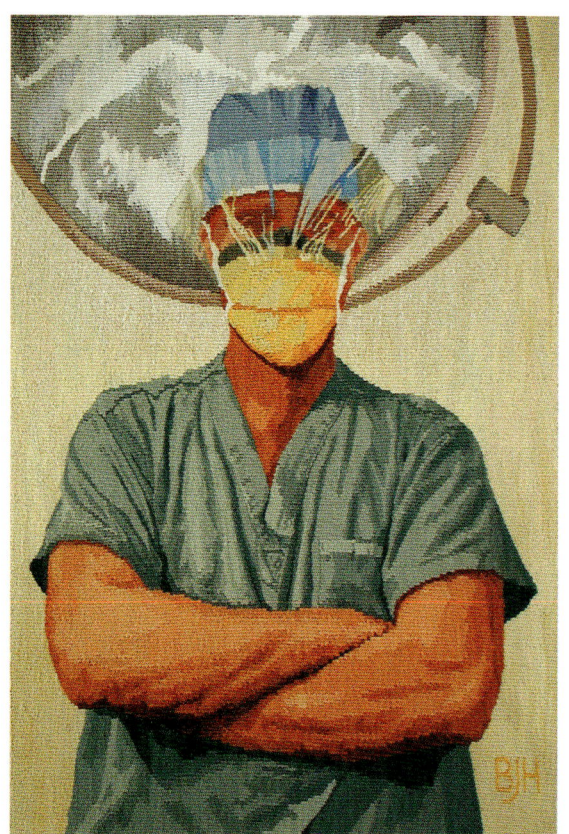 

Cover-Ups: The Surgeon
Barbara Heller, 2002–2003 | 35" × 25" | Wool, cotton, rayon (most hand dyed); linen warp

One of Heller's series in which clothing covers the face completely. Once the face is masked, the mood can turn mysterious, even sinister. Some cloth no longer invites touch.

Cover-Ups: Canadian Klansman
Barbara Heller, 2000 | 35" × 25" | Wool, cotton, rayon (most hand-dyed); linen warp

Other pieces include a crossing guard, women in burkas, a bride.

Erosion
Michael Rohde, 2008 | 36" × 38" | Wool, indigo dye | Photo: Andrew Newhart

Inspired by a Tibetan belt, old and deteriorating. A reminder, perhaps, of what is happening in Tibet now.

Failure to Communicate
Patricia Williams, 2013 | 44.5" × 59"| Wool; seine twine cotton warp

Reminiscent of the three monkeys, who see, hear, and speak no evil.

Each woman is differentiated from the others—even their clothing doesn't agree. These heads are satisfyingly large.

Running Shoe
Deann Rubin, 1988 | 10" × 10"

Embellished with a weaver's lines, stripes, and dots. A profusion of different techniques producing a result that is very nearly pure pattern.

The Sweater
Annika Ekdahl, 1995 | 7'4.5" × 6'6.75" | Wool | Collection of Malmö City Museum | Photo: Matilda Thulin, Malmö Museer

The size of this tapestry provokes awe. Viewers might otherwise imagine it on their own bodies. The color work is rich and intense, drifting away from the object itself into the field of white.

The Ancestor's Garment
Designed by Yael Lurie | Woven by Jean Pierre Larochette, 2004–13 | 48" × 20" (× 2) | Wool, silk, mercerized cotton; cotton warp

The garment in this piece is a *huipil*. Weeping faces reside amid the roses; stylized tears appear at the foot of each diamond. Larochette is the fourth generation of tapestry weavers in his French family. Lurie and Larochette stand out as one of the few couples in the world working together as designer and weaver, a partnership of more than 50 years.

The Migdale Kilt
Joan Baxter, 2008 | 31.5" × 83.5" | Wool

The faint tartan on this kilt merges into its winter Scottish landscape.

Eight
HISTORICAL SELF-REFERENCE

The tapestries in this chapter refer back to earlier tapestries and their aesthetic worlds—from content to technique to iconography.

THE RANGE OF TAPESTRY STYLES

Combining visual traditions can provide a theme all on its own. These next two pieces combine several conventions.

From Flemish to Finnish
Suzanne Fitzgerald, 2014–15 | 7.5" × 12" | Mixed fibers, applied beads; cotton warp

From left to right: a Flemish rabbit, a South American burro, a William Morris bird, Finnish flowers, and writing.

Joseph's Questions
Mary Lane, 2002 | 34" × 34.5" | Wool, cotton, silk; cotton warp

A collage of details from various extant cultures—Norwegian *billedvev* (Norwegian for "tapestry") in the center, Kuba raffia cloth (Kuba cloth has its origin in the Democratic Republic of Congo), an American quilt, a Persian compound twill. The script is intentionally illegible.

Lane knew someone who was seeking his roots.

Some weavers make visual reference to particular tapestry types, such as Navajo rugs or Asian kilims.

EYE DAZZLERS

Germantown Eye Dazzler, ca. 1890s
7'3" × 5'1" | Cotton, wool, dovetailed tapestry weave | Robert Allerton Endowment | Art Institute of Chicago

(contemporary reworking) (with an eye!)
Marlowe Katoney, 2013 | Germantown three-ply wool | Private collection | Photo: Todd Roth

CHIEF'S BLANKET

Chief's Blanket, 3rd phase, 1860–65
4'9" × 5'8.5" | Wool, single interlocking tapestry weave; twined edges; corner tassel | Robert Allerton Endowment | Art Institute of Chicago

The Chair series
Janusz Kozikowski, 1987 | 47" × 47" | Wool

Here the Chief's Blanket defines the unseen chair.

SENNEH

Senneh, Persian Kilim, detail
(about one-third of the whole—which measures 5' × 9') | Wool

A kilim handwoven by Kurds who live in or around the town of Senneh (now more properly Sanandaj) in western Iran. These kilims are prized for their delicate pattern, coloring, and fine weave.

Opus I: Persiche Variationen / Persian Variations
Ulrich and Antje Reimkasten, 1982 | 5'8" × 3'5" | Wool; black cotton warp | Photo: Bernd Kunert

Echoes, to some extent, Senneh kilims, in which the huge numbers of details play such an essential part. Here, the figures epitomize a relentlessly harsh world.

Some weavers refer visually to contemporary tapestries.

For many years, Archie Brennan (and Susan Martin Maffei) taught tapestry weavers in monthly sessions—the Wednesday group. One day Brennan proposed that weavers should try exploring the space between two bosc pears against a horizon line. Part of what inspired Anna Byrd Mays was a piece by Brennan, #XIV in his group called *At a Window*.

Three Pears Talking / At a Window XIV
Archie Brennan, 1995 | 12.5" × 12" | Wool, cotton

Brennan said that the idea for his tapestry arose from a Thomas Keneally novel, about a woman who loved gossip and let it ripen like fruit in a window.

Pairs
Anna Byrd Mays, 2014 | 14" × 10" (× 4) | Cotton, wool

Mays said that the challenge "has grown into an obsession and a rather large body of work as cloth and on paper."

EUROPEAN IMAGERY

In the fifteenth century, tapestries from Switzerland and Germany were populated by wild human figures. The imagery appears liberating rather than evil. The term "green man" was coined in the twentieth century to include this kind of figure.

Wild Men and Wild Women, 1430–70
Switzerland | 1'3" × 9' | Wool | © Victoria and Albert Museum, London

Here a wild man is bearded, and a wild woman shows off her breasts through gaps in the body-covering leaves. They are accompanied by fabulous beasts.

Le Bal des Sauvages / Le Bal Ardents | The Ball of Wild People / The Fiery Ball, 15th century
9'9" × 16'5" | Wool, silk | Château of Saumur | Photo: Richard Godrant

A French version of the *wild men and women*, recording a historical event in 1393, during the reign of Charles VI. At a formal costume ball, the king danced with five noble ladies who wore leaves, breast holes and all. A highly volatile glue attached the leaves to their bodies. Tragedy ensued when the glue caught fire from a torch brought to the scene by the king's brother.

Topsham Observance
Pat Johns, 1986 | 3'6" × 5" | Hand-dyed wool

One of many artworks commissioned by the British group Common Ground. Through individual parish maps such as this, which shows the part of the county of Devon where the Exe and the Clyst Rivers meet, the group hoped to provide people with a visual reminder of the world around them, urging them to take greater care of their environment. Johns was the sole tapestry weaver invited to participate. The green man is associated with the earth itself.

Johns wrote the verse and wove it in, she says, so that the green man wouldn't take over.

La Musique / Music
Designed by Marc Saint Saens | Atelier Tabard Frères et Soeurs, Aubusson, 1951 | 8'6" × 17' | Wool | L'Abbatoir Fine Arts Museum, Toulouse | Photo: © Adagp, Paris, Richard Godrant

The figures filled with leaves standing on the right side of the tapestry hint at another possible identity for *wild people*, that of Adam and Eve.

Adam and Eve
Maryam Hermina, 1965 | 4'7" × 7'10" | Wool; cotton warp

Hermina was among the first generations of young artists in the Ramses Wissa Wassef Art Centre, near Cairo. Since its founding in 1951, the workshop has offered young Egyptians the opportunity to create, mostly tapestries. Intentionally, no formal training is offered, since founder Wissa Wassef, an architect, was convinced that children would be able to figure it out on their own. The tapestries are world famous.

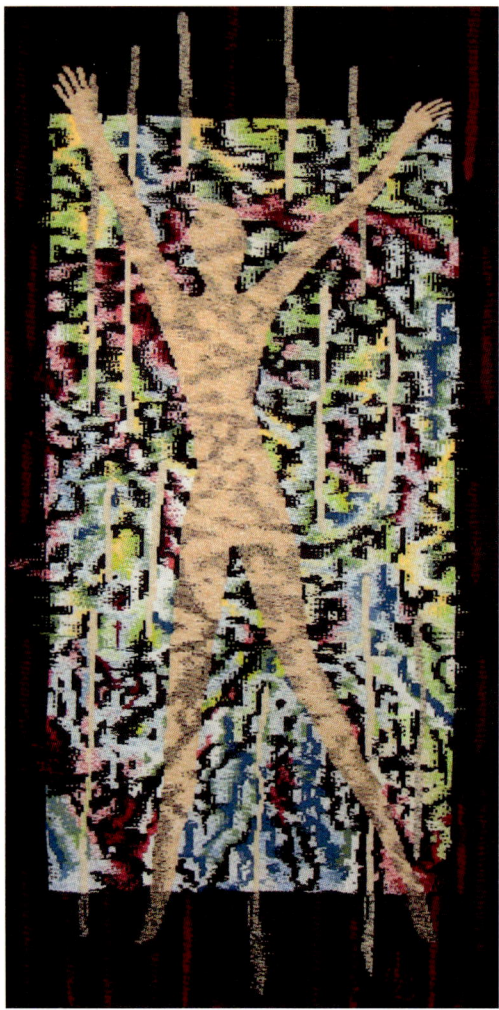

If I Could
Liliana Crespi, 2011 | 5'4" × 2'10" | Wool; cotton warp

The body stretches upward against a garden, whose vines encircle it, becoming part of its patterning.

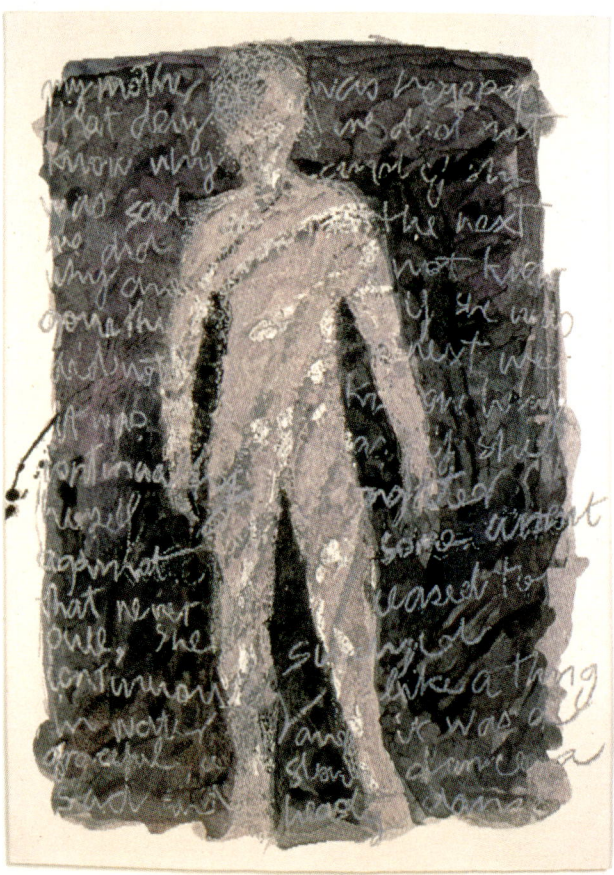

Daughter
Kay Lawrence, 1995–96 | 6'4" × 4'7" | Wool, cotton, linen; cotton warp

Here, Lawrence has filled the body (and the field of the tapestry) with words like journal entries, part of an unending dialogue with a teenaged daughter.

Some weavers are inspired by particular individual tapestries—or series—and they reweave them in a contemporary idiom.

FEAST

Herodes Gjestebud / The Feast of Herod, 1613–1750
6'4" × 4'9" | Wool; linen warp | Norsk Folkesmuseum, Oslo

Everybody in the tapestry, ready to consume the food before them, reads as flat (rather than dimensional), like wallpaper.

Barockfesten / A Baroque Dinner Party
Annika Ekdahl, 2000 | 10'6" × 9'9" | Wool; linen warp

Again, all highly individual people, flattened around this large table, with a huge summer pudding in the middle. Ekdahl has also included a frame around the frame around the table.

A Meeting of the Members of the Board
Archie Brennan | 5'4" × 3'3" | Wool, linen, cotton; cotton warp

Brennan specifically cited the visual qualities of the *Herod's Feast* as inspiration for what he wove, choosing the participants from his own sketches of people interviewed on the news program *Nightline*. No food, though—just cigarettes and glasses of water. The even writing around the edge manages, as though effortlessly, to leave room for AB, Brennan's signature.

LA DAME À LA LICORNE / THE LADY AND THE UNICORN

In this six-piece group, woven in Flanders, each of the first five is devoted to one of the five senses—and a last piece to the giving up of the sensual. The series is held in the collection of the Paris Medieval Museum, the Cluny. They were made in approximately 1500, of wool and silk.

La Dame à la Licorne—le goût / The Lady and the Unicorn: Taste (detail)
11'11" × 10'7" (the whole)

Mille Fleurs Misery
Lynn Mayne, 2005 | 23" × 22"| Wool, cotton, metallic thread

Mayne, who has intense allergies, has reimagined a woman amid the fields of flowers. She did a second piece, based on *smell*, called *Unicorn Dander?*, with a maiden about to sneeze.

EIGHT

La Dame à la Licorne—la vue / The Lady and the Unicorn: Sight (detail)
10'2" × 10'10" (the whole)

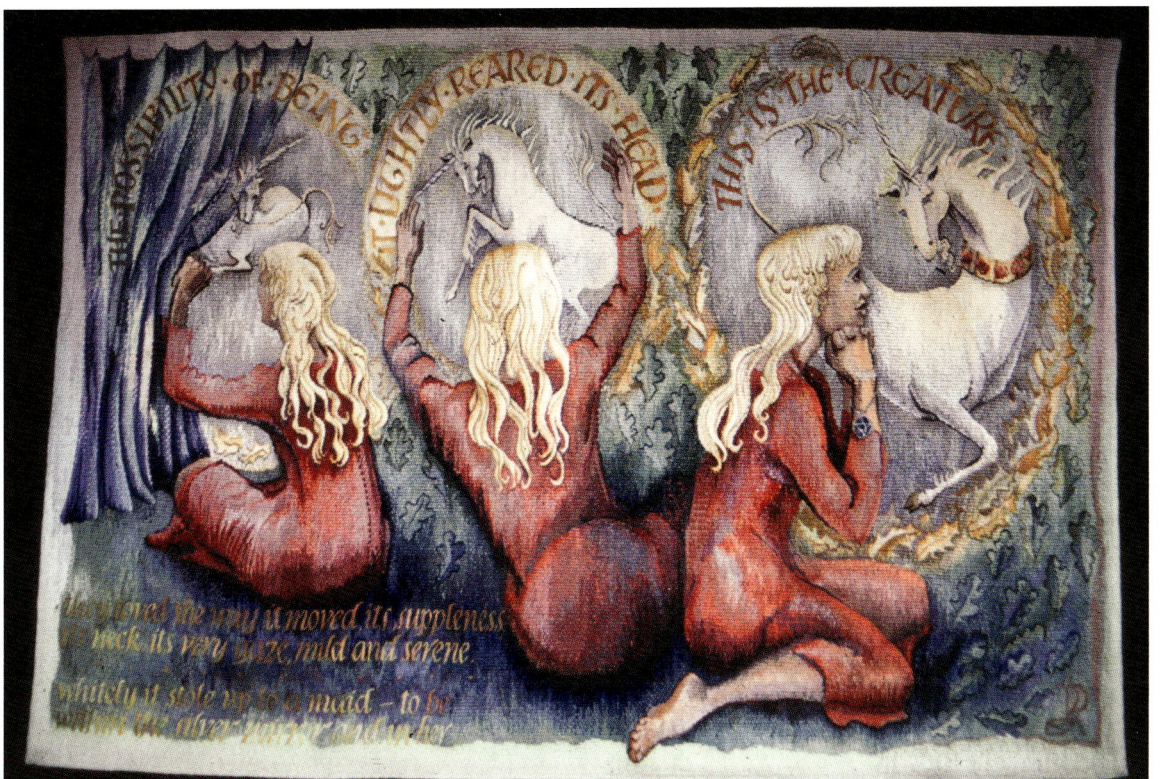

The Unicorn Tapestry
Pat Johns, 1990 | 3'3" × 5' | Hand-dyed wool

In this piece, a maiden looks beyond this world to the unicorn, who is called "a possibility of being." As the images move from left to right, both the girl and the unicorn grow larger.

Ilossa / In Joy
Aino Kajaniemi, 2013 | 4'9" × 5'2" | Linen, cotton, wool, viscose

The unicorn as a source of pure delight. Is this the circus?

L'OFFRANDE DU COEUR /
THE OFFERING OF THE HEART

L'Offrande du Coeur / The Offering of the Heart, 1400–10

8'2" × 6'10" | Wool, silk | Louvre

The lover offers his heart, which looks like a Valentine candy. Stylized leaves emphasize the rhythms of weaving.

The Offering of the Heart

Lynne Curran, 1993 | 13" × 10" | Linen, silk, cotton, fine wool | Private collection

The heart has become a strawberry, but, in this case, it's the woman's gift to the man. Other hearts appear in the border and in the curves of the wire bench back. Curran's distinctive weaving style creates innumerable textures.

LA CHASSE À LA LICORNE / THE HUNT OF THE UNICORN

A group of seven tapestries (including fragments), woven at the beginning of the fifteenth century in the southern Netherlands. It now hangs at the Cloisters branch of the Metropolitan Museum of Art.

The Hunt of the Unicorn—the Hunters Enter the Woods, 1495–1505
12'1" × 10'4" | Wool, silk, silver gilt threads; wool warp

The Hunt of the Unicorn
Vita Gelúniene | Photo: R. Scerbauskas

Here the two realistic figures with their dog, set into the *mille fleurs* setting, seem to be on a shopping expedition, with that exquisitely rendered paper bag. The man—oh my!—has a windup key in his back. The cupids below appear to sit on potty chairs. What else is unexpected?

EIGHT

210

The Hunt of the Unicorn—the Mystic Capture of the Unicorn, 1495–1505

5'6" × 2'1" | Wool, silk, silver gilt threads; wool warp

It is said that only a virgin can lure the unicorn to its capture or death.

In this fragment, the maiden looks sly.

The Mystic Hunt of the Unicorn

Woven by the West Dean Tapestry Studio for Stirling Castle, Scotland | 2011–14 | Weaving team (which changed over the three years of weaving): Caron Penney, Katherine Swailes, Louise Martin, Rudi Richardson, Jennifer Bennett, Alison Baxter, Ruth Jones, Emma Jo Webster, Louise Trotter | 10'10" × 4'7" | Wool, mercerized cotton, gold thread with cotton core; cotton warp

In this segment, designed by Katherine Swailes, the surviving fragments have been reworked into a whole.

Hand to Hand
Cecilia Blomberg, 2009 | 9" × 9" | Wool, linen, metallic; seine twine warp

The weaver's contemporary hand meets the hand of the maiden. For a time, Blomberg worked with the team from the West Dean Tapestry Studio.

Princess Di Meets a Medieval Maiden
Archie Brennan, 1980s | 38" × 42" | Wool, silk

Brennan speculated about how the concept of beauty shifts. Over time, the medieval maiden has suffered a change as the white of her skin yellowed. White does not stay white. What would Princess Di have looked like in the years to come?

The Hunt of the Unicorn—the Unicorn in Captivity, 1495–1505
12' × 8'4" | Wool, silk, silver gilt threads; wool warp

Bitter Harvest
Murray Gibson, 1991 | 5' × 2'10" | Wool, silk, gold

The most obvious visual reference is the tree within a fence, from the *Unicorn in Captivity*. But in this tree, each apple (pomegranates in the historical tapestry) is labeled with the Latin term for each of the seven deadly sins. The red-and-blue fields echo the ground colors in the Apocalypse tapestries. (The stylized water calls to mind specifically *La Nouvelle Jerusalem / The New Jerusalem* episode in that series.) In addition, hard to read in a reproduction, the field is composed of diamond shapes, like kilim patterns. On close examination, one finds rats spewing golden flames.

When asked to talk about the work, Gibson, who wove it during an artist residency in New York City, said it was hard to live in such an intensely urban place.

HEROINES

Queen Semiramis with Attendants, ca. 1480
Tournai, Flanders | 8'3" × 8'5" | Wool, silk | Honolulu Museum of Art | Gift of Charles M. and Anna C. Cooke Trust, 1946

Queen of the Assyrians from ca. 800 BCE. One of several tapestries devoted to heroines. Another, *Penthisilea*, belongs to the collection at the Château of Angers.

Marianne North, a Vision of Eden

(from the series *Intrepid Women: A Celebration of Women Travellers*) | Joanna Buxton, 1985 | 4' × 4' | New Zealand wool, mercerized and unmercerized cotton, silk, all hand-dyed; cotton warp

North was a Victorian plant hunter and prolific botanical painter. The plant-dense frame is noteworthy.

Buxton made about half a dozen of these *intrepid women*.

Gertrude Bell, Daughter of the Desert

(from the series *Intrepid Women: A Celebration of Women Travellers*) | Joanna Buxton, 1983 | 5' × 6'8" | New Zealand wool, mercerized and unmercerized cotton, silk, all hand-dyed; cotton warp

Bell was an English political administrator and traveler to Arabian countries in the late 19th and early 20th centuries.

THE FATES

The Triumph of Death, or The Three Fates, fragment, early 16th century
South Netherlands | Wool, silk | © Victoria and Albert Museum, London

The three fates in Greek mythology are Clotho, who spins the thread of life; Lachesis, who measures it (the allotter); and Atropos, who cuts it, ending the life. The three are thus intensely associated with textiles. (The prone body is that of Chastity.)

Triumph of . . . Whatever
Peter Harris, 1996 | 5' × 8' | Wool; linen warp

During the Renaissance, tapestries often imitated painting, an ideal less than satisfactory to today's weavers. Harris has taken Breughel's *The Triumph of Death*, with its visual references to the Fates (the woman in the upper right, clutching the spool).

Three Fates
Henry Moore, designer | West Dean Tapestry Studio, 1983–84 | Weavers: Pat Taylor and Fiona Abercromby | 8' 8" × 11'6" | Linen, wool; cotton warp

Atropos stands in the middle, ready to cut.

Commissions such as this one, to weave Henry Moore drawings, enabled the establishment of the West Dean Studio in 1976.

The Three Fates
Murray Gibson, 2002 | *Left to right:* Clotho, Lachesis, Atropos | 1'6" × 6' overall | Wool, cotton | Collection of the Canada Council Art Bank, Ottawa, Canada

Gibson changes what happens—and with grim whimsy. Clotho spins a top, Lachesis plays a game of cat's cradle, but Atropos still cuts the thread, though her scissors are fingers.

The River Wyrd
Sarah Swett, 2004 | 48" × 36" | Wool

Wyrd is a concept in Anglo-Saxon culture roughly corresponding to fate. Rivers are often associated with time. Swett blends Anglo-Saxon and Greek traditions here. Each sister carries out her role. The weaver cannot resist clothing her sisters in shorts—a contemporary touch. She weaves several frames, some of which blend into landscapes.

PENELOPE

Penelope at Her Loom
Fragment from *The Story of Penelope and the Story of the Cimbri Women* from the series *The Stories of Virtuous Women*, 1480–83 | French or Franco-Flemish | 59" × 39.4" | Wool | Boston Museum of Fine Arts

Penelope may be the patron saint of tapestry weavers. She weaves all day and unweaves all night. It is said that *unweaving* is known as the *Penelope stitch*. The Latin along the bottom reads: *I will always be the wife to Ulysses.*

Await. Penelope

Celina Grigore, 1998 | 5'10" × 6'8" | Wool, silk; cotton warp

As though every time Penelope begins to weave again, some other pattern of cloth emerges.

Penelope Revisited

Archie Brennan

In this piece, one sees the illusion of weaving—and unweaving. The warp is a woven representation of warp—not warp left unwoven.

Penelope
Ben Hymers, 2016 | Wool; cotton warp

Perhaps Penelope has made a tent of cloth, with hourglasses, to show all she weaves. And what to say about her crossed bare legs?

Penelope at her loom has also inspired self-awareness among weavers.

Me at Loom
Mieko Konaka, 2007 | 19.5" × 19.5"

So, Who's in Charge Here?
Sarah Swett, 2001 | 12" × 12" |
Handspun wool, silk; wool warp, natural dyes

A very clever use of actual warp. In weaving, the weaver creates herself.

HISTORICAL SELF-REFERENCE

Nine
THE ART IN THE CLOTH

This book begins with an image that reads *NOT PAINT*, thus calling attention to itself as a piece of cloth. Here, at the end—on the facing page—is another work, one that includes a painted detail on top of the woven surface. Once again, the tapestry calls attention to the elements of its construction.

The painted section is known as *potomage*, a technique that can be found in historical Chinese and Japanese work, as well as some German and Swiss pieces. (In the European tapestries, faces are sometimes blank because the paint has flaked off.)

If Penelope is the patron saint of tapestry, she might also be the patron saint of insomnia. Here the weaver sleeps.

The painted part is the face and hands. Since painting has traditionally been labeled art and weaving craft, the weaver is making a wry—and useful—commentary: no art without craft.

Art Sleeps in Craft
Grace Eckert, 1983 | 5'7" × 3'1" | Wool, linen; linen warp; paint | Life-sized